# Beginner's Needlecraft

# Beginner's

# Needlecraft

ANNETTE FELDMAN

Harper & Row, Publishers

New York, Evanston, San Francisco, London

Other books by Annette Feldman

KNIT, PURL, AND DESIGN!

CROCHET AND CREATIVE DESIGN

FIRST EDITION

*Designed by Gwendolyn O. England*

Library of Congress Cataloging in Publication Data

Feldman, Annette.
   Beginner's needlecraft.
   1. Needlework. 2. Fancy work. I. Title.
TT750.F43     746.4     73–14259
ISBN 0–06–011232–8

To VIRGINIA S. MANN

needlework editor and good friend

# Contents

APPLIQUÉ

Patterns for cutting flowers and butterflies and a charming dressed-up wiggle-worm. You are told how to whip-stitch your cutouts onto simple things, turning these items into delightful, individually designed creations. In this chapter you will learn how to add a personal touch to a show towel, a tablecloth, a child's dress, and a scarf.

CREWEL EMBROIDERY

A few basic stitches and, with these stitches, you are taught how to make a decorative paneled table screen, a book cover, and a wall hanging, all worked in shades of blue and in patterns closely resembling those appearing so often in ancient Chinese art forms.

CROCHETING

A group of designs made up of gay textured stripes and the popular little multicolored granny squares. The beauty of the designs belies the fact that only the very simple single and half-double crochet stitches were used to make them.

KNITTING

Instructions for a lady's cap and vest, a classic ribbed slipover, and a man's sleeveless cardigan—all of which can be made with just the basic knit and purl stitches. Directions for knitting the garments are written in a wide range of sizes.

# A Tale about Needlework

Many of today's needlecraft leisure arts are derived from primitive man's ingenuity in devising means of using a few raw materials to make some of the things he urgently needed for his existence. He early learned to use earth clays to build his hut and to rub stones together to make the fire over which he cooked his food. He fashioned his clothes from the various natural fibers available to him, and soon found means to decorate them. This was the earliest use of the needlework arts.

When fishermen in very ancient times began knotting strands of fiber together, it was certainly not with the thought of indulging in an interesting new hobby with which to while away spare time. They had little spare time, and the thought of knotting one length of fiber to another came about only as they tried to find ways of making nets large enough to haul in a sufficient supply of fish from the sea to be able to feed themselves, their families, and the people in their community. They certainly didn't anticipate that centuries later sailors would be using their knots for making lanyards of hemp and rope with which to hold spars and cargo in place. Nor could these ancient fishermen possibly have envisioned that the technique they had developed for their own survival would become popular in the 20th century as the fun craft of macramé.

Others of our fun crafts were also started long, long ago by those who were shrewd enough and pressured enough by necessity to take advantage of whatever materials were available. Legend and historical bits of real evidence tell us that the earliest known practice of knitting dates to the 4th century B.C. Only recently there were found, in an Egytian tomb dating to that time, a well-preserved pair of hand-knit socks. Archeologists believe that the capability of making such well-fashioned socks came about after years of practice, long after someone first realized that the use of a strand of fiber and some kind of tool to work it around (probably four fingers on the left hand) made it possible to produce lengths of woven goods with which to clothe himself.

Patchwork is another of today's popular leisure crafts that had a very humble beginning, not quite so ancient as macramé and knitting, but like them born of the necessity of survival. The early American colonists had few means of protecting themselves against the long cold New England winters, and it was they who started and developed this type of work. Unable to buy blankets to cover themselves with while in bed or hangings to put over their windows and doors to keep out the icy drafts, they ingeniously put together good little bits and pieces cut from their worn-out clothing to make the large pieces they needed to keep themselves warm.

The needlecrafts we've mentioned thus far began as very basic and functional work, but other crafts such as crewel embroidery and appliqué were inspired solely by man's desire to add beauty and embellishment to the things he possessed and to his way of life. Crocheting, too, started as a decorative art, a form of lace-making and a delicate decoration. Ladies of the upper classes during the Renaissance occupied many of their leisure hours crocheting lovely things with which to adorn themselves and their homes. Ironically, however, this so-called luxury art, started as a means of creating a dainty kind of finery, served at one time as a means of survival for a very large group of people. In the mid-nineteenth century when the potato crops failed in Ireland, famine and financial disaster devastated the country. English ladies who had been busying themselves with the new fashion of crocheting wanted to help their neighbors in some way, and it occurred to them that the Irish women might be able to put this skill to good use as an income-producing cottage industry. They taught them what they knew about crocheting, and the Irish women did indeed make a great success of their new industry and helped themselves to overcome their plight. Working with fine linen thread

and their new little crochet hooks, they created many new and very exciting patterns of their own. *Irish crochet* is still one of the most beautiful of laces, imaginative and intricate in design and very skillfully executed.

As interesting as the tales to be told about handcrafts are, perhaps the most interesting one of all would be the one that could truly describe the compelling fascination of all the handcraft arts. People have always enjoyed doing needlework, and today more people than ever, both men and women and young and old, are finding pleasure in it. There is something wonderful about using our two hands to make one little stitch follow another toward the final composition of a lovely creation of our own. We certainly do not need to make our things any more, for stores are filled with goods these days and we can buy practically anything we want. There are strong reasons, however, why we still choose to make our own hand-knits and hand-crochets and hand-embroidered pieces. The needs that we want to meet are no longer those of basic existence, but the very important ones of relaxation and of a certain fulfillment within ourselves. We can satisfy these psychological wants by creating our own things, so easy to make with some yarn and a needle or hook of some kind.

Tension runs high these days, and although most of us are caught up to some degree in the high-speed pace of life, most of us seem also to be in search of some kind of a battle weapon against its pressures. Innately we feel that things are going too fast, and though we must keep up with them to survive, during the many extra leisure hours we have gained because of the mechanization of our world, we keep looking for something quiet and very special to do. The rhythmic, soft clicking of a pair of knitting needles seems to calm our nerves and fill our emotional needs, as does the working, space by space, through the open mesh of a large piece of canvas with a small latchet hook and a few strands of yarn.

Maybe it is that slow, easy steadiness involved in the working of the various crafts that appeals to us most; or maybe the euphoric calm that descends upon us as we become absorbed in the gradual unfolding of some beautiful stitch-by-stitch object that we've chosen to make. It is not at all unusual these days to watch a racing, roaring, space-age television show, and at the same time be thoroughly involved with the gentle plying of a blunt-edged needle threaded with yarn through a piece of canvas mesh, quietly drawing a beautiful needlepoint picture. Indeed, it is not unusual either if this piece of work is a lovely pastoral scene, in very direct contrast to the hustle-bustle of the television program.

Another reason more and more people have taken to the needle-art crafts is that the new designs and the new things to make are so very attractive. Stores abound with beautiful yarns and fabrics and patterns, and many persons have been lured just by looking at them into wanting to try something for themselves. Certainly there are many explanations for people being so very busy with hobbies these days, but there is one special reason that we would like to mention, and this is one we hope will encourage you to join the fold of happy needle-art craftsmen, if you have not already done so. A 17th century clergyman, Mr. Isaac Watts, admonished those who frittered away their time in the following way: "Satan finds some mischief still for idle hands to do." This seems to be a negative way of saying what we want to say: "Busy Hands Are Bless'd."

# Welcome to All Beginners!

This book is written for those who have never done needlework before, and also for those who have perhaps enjoyed working with one of the crafts and would like to learn another. We know that you will enjoy many pleasantly rewarding hours of fun and relaxation in whichever of the crafts you attempt.

Some of you already know which of the various media interests you most, while others are not quite sure but know only that they do want to do some kind of handwork. In the pages following we describe several of today's most popular crafts. Those who know what they want to work at have only to turn to the pages featuring that particular craft to find some very lovely patterns with simple, easy-to-follow directions and all the other information that you need to know to get started.

For those, however, who are not quite sure of just where to begin, we suggest that, before de-

ciding, you browse through the various chapters, looking at the designs and reading through the General Instructions for each kind of work. By doing this you will easily be able to tell what type of things can be made in each medium and what the general working procedure is. Although all the handcrafts are easy enough for anyone to learn, there are certain differences in the way each is worked and therefore reasons why one would perhaps have more appeal for you than another. If you are a "sewing person," for example, you might be much happier attempting a project involving appliqué or patchwork rather than one worked with a crochet hook or a pair of knitting needles; and if you like to work with broader strokes, then either latchet hooking or macramé would be interesting for you to try.

As people have many personalities, so the various needle arts have "personalities," too. Beautiful things can be made in each of the handcrafts, but you will see, by reading the General Instructions, that some require more attention to detail than do others, that some require concentration while others are "social," and that some go quickly and others are more painstaking and require more patience. All are fun, but if you have any doubt as to which you would like to try, consider matching "personalities."

The choice of things to make in any of the crafts is practically limitless, and while we cannot show very many in this book, we have tried to cover various categories such as clothing and accessories and things for the home. Once you have mastered whichever technique you have chosen to learn, you will be able to make many additional things by using designs from current periodicals or creating your own. Almost any art can be applied to the making of almost anything, and the sense of fulfillment you get in actually making the things will be as great as the pleasure you will derive from using them, or from perhaps presenting them to those who would be overjoyed to receive a gift that you personally made especially for them.

We hope that you will start soon on whatever it is that interests you most. But whatever it is you do start on, there are a few rules that you should be aware of before you set out on your actual project. These simple, specific rules are outlined in each chapter, in addition to the very commonsense ones of working with good materials, in a good light, in a comfortably relaxed position, and in an organized sort of way that will assure you of a good finished product and, equally important, of good working habits in whatever other projects you may attempt later on. You will be happy for having started the right way, and we will be happy for having taught you how to achieve master craftsmanship so that whatever you attempt will completely satisfy the anticipation you have in wanting to create something beautiful.

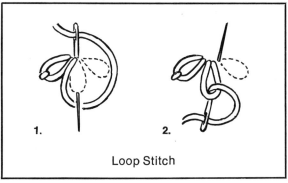

**Loop Stitch**

Bring yarn through at bottom of petal on traced line, then loop yarn and pass needle back through fabric, bringing it up at center top of petal with yarn under needle (1). Make a small stitch over the loop and pass needle through fabric, bringing it up at bottom of next petal (2).

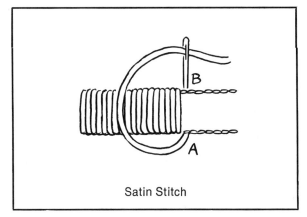

**Satin Stitch**

Bring yarn through at **A** on traced line, then pass needle down through fabric at same place on opposite traced line at **B.** Carry needle across back of material, pass through fabric at point next to **A** and continue to work in same manner as first stitch.

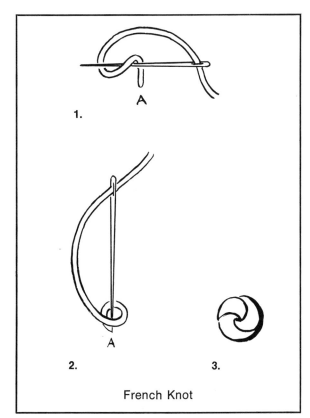

**French Knot**

Bring yarn through at dot on **A,** wrap yarn around needle once (as shown) or as many times as desired (1), then pass needle down through fabric at point **A** (2). Completed stitch looks as shown (3).

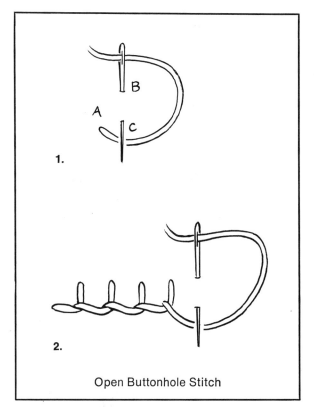

**Open Buttonhole Stitch**

Bring yarn through at **A** on traced line, pass needle through fabric from **B** to **C** (1). Continue working in this manner along traced line to completion of stitch (2).

## GENERAL INSTRUCTIONS

First *plan* your design and the fabric and colors you want to use. The amount of material you need will be small, but it is good to have whatever you have decided to use on hand and ready to be put into work.

Trace off the pattern or patterns you will be using, then paste your tracings onto cardboard and cut them out to be used as pattern pieces.

Place your pattern pieces on the fabric you will be using for them and cut your material, leaving a ⅛-inch allowance around the entire outer edge. This allowance will be turned under when you stitch your appliqué onto the piece to be trimmed. *Exception:* If you are going to embroider your pattern in place, cut the piece along the tracing line. Do *not* leave the ⅛-inch allowance. Pin the piece in place and use an open buttonhole stitch if you are embroidering by hand,

or the appliqué stitch if you are embroidering by machine.

Put your fabric piece wrong side up on your ironing board (your pattern piece on top), then press the seam-allowance portion over your pattern piece. By doing this, you will be easily able to follow your turn-under guideline when stitching the piece in place.

Pin all your pieces into the positions in which you want them to be sewn.

Where a curved edge appears on a piece, snip lightly into the piece (not quite all the way up to the guideline). This will keep your piece from puckering when you stitch it into place.

Turn your ⅛-inch seam allowance to the underside, then stitch your pieces in place. Where the edge of one piece is overlapped by another piece, it is not necessary to turn under the portion of that edge which is covered.

# Butterfly Scarf

# Beginner's Needlecraft

# Appliqué

Each of the handcraft skills in this book is different from the others in both its working method and the end result it produces. It is for these reasons that the art of appliqué, like all the others, has its own special appeal for a certain type of person. Appliqué is a trimming art, and the persons who enjoy it most are those who like to do a little simple sewing, and to use their own ingenuity and creative ability to embellish and add color and adornment to already existing things which are perhaps a little plain.

It is not hard to do appliqué, nor is it a precision art which requires a great deal of patience and concentration. A few hours of work and a little imagination can create most pleasing results. The applying of an attractive pattern or group of patterns to an ordinary dress, blouse, tablecloth, or anything else can enhance it and change it into a highly original and very attractive creation.

Appliqué is done basically by placing cut-out fabric motifs onto the material of the piece you are going to trim and then stitching them into place. Any type of pattern form can be used for appliquéing, as well as any kind of material and any kind of stitching to set the pattern in place.

You can make your own trim by tracing off your pattern form from a picture of a pretty flower in a magazine, or cutting out the blossoms on a piece of printed fabric, or just cutting a few geometric shapes of your own design. You can use plain or printed material, or mix the two. The choice of stitching is also completely your own. You may whip-stitch your design into place, machine-stitch it, or use any interesting embroidery stitch. A combination of a few different stitches

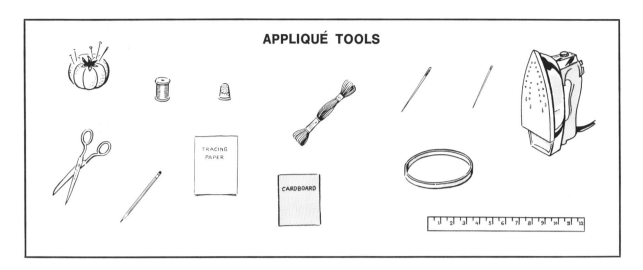

## APPLIQUÉ TOOLS

adds interest to a design. If your sewing is not perfectly precise or regular, this is all right too, and may even, with its irregularities, add a more creative look to your finished piece.

The patterns offered here are examples of some of the ways in which appliqué work can enhance a simple, basic item, and the things we have chosen to trim are purely suggestive. You may want to use the same type of background items or you may prefer other things, perhaps a pillowcase, a bedspread, or an apron. Your own aesthetic sense will tell you whether to use the design as it is shown, or repeat it several times over and in different formations and colors, thus creating an interesting pattern within a group of patterns. There is great leeway in making appliqué designs, and that is perhaps one of the main reasons why people enjoy this craft so much.

## APPLIQUÉ STITCHES

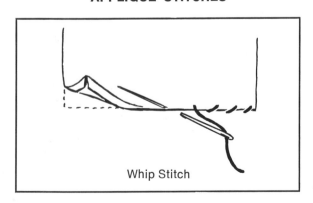

Whip Stitch

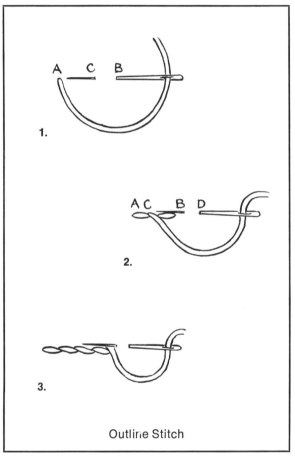

Outline Stitch

Bring yarn through at **A** on traced line, pass needle through fabric from **B** to **C** (1), then pass needle through fabric from **D** to **B** (2). Continue working in this manner to completion of stitch (3).

## MATERIALS

7-inch square of orange Dacron or polyester cotton
1 long white chiffon scarf
1 package yellow baby rickrack
6-strand embroidery floss in orange, brown, black, and yellow
1 package small gold sequins

Trace off the butterfly, then cut out the trace-off for your pattern piece. Pin the pattern piece onto the material and trace around the edge. Pencil in lightly all markings shown on the butterfly design. Cut out along the traced edge. Pin the cut material in desired position on the scarf. Stitch to the scarf with orange embroidery floss and a closely placed buttonhole stitch, following the dotted lines around the outside edges. Stitch rickrack in place along the long dotted lines on the top wings. Embroider the body in brown satin stitch, the antennae in brown outline stitch, and the two elongated spots on the lower wings in yellow outline stitch. Stitch sequins in place on the round spots on wings. Using double strands of black embroidery floss, embroider an outline stitch along the top curved section of the lower wing, stitching just above the orange open buttonhole stitch.

# Hand Towel with Flower Motif

## MATERIALS

1 white terry hand towel, 1 yellow washcloth

8-inch square of white piqué or Indianhead for
the flower, a small piece of green material
for the leaves, and a small piece of yellow
for the center of flower

6-strand embroidery floss in desired color for
outlining the flower

Trace off the flower and the center of the flower
along the outside edge, then cut out the trace-
offs and use them for pattern pieces. Trace off
the leaf in the same manner. Pin the pattern
pieces onto the materials to be used, and trace
around the edges. Mark the dotted lines as shown
on the flower design for petals and work over
them with embroidery floss and an outline stitch.
Cut out the flower along the traced edge, and
the center and the 2 leaves ⅛ inch beyond the
traced edge. Turn under the ⅛-inch allowance
of the center piece and the leaves, and baste on
the wrong side of the work, clipping in around
the curves so that the pieces will not pucker when
sewn in place.

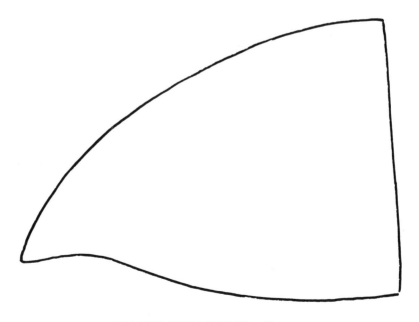

Pin the center piece onto the flower, whip-stitch it in place, then pull out the basting thread. Pin the flower and leaves in place on the towel as shown. Whip-stitch the leaves in place, then pull out the basting thread. Pin the flower in place (do *not* turn under the outside edges of this piece). Leaving a 5- or 6-inch opening at the top for the pocket, stitch the flower to the towel with embroidery floss and a closely placed button-hole stitch, starting at the beginning of the open edge and working around to the other side of the opening, then continuing to embroider around the open portion to the starting point.

Place yellow washcloth in pocket.

# Child's Dress

## MATERIALS

Child's dress of any desired size

¾ yard green ball fringe for the worm's body and trim around the neck

Small piece of ecru material for the stem and underside of the mushroom, red dotted material for the mushroom cap, pink for the worm's head and yellow for the butterfly

6-strand embroidery floss in yellow, brown, green, and black

Trace off each portion of the design separately—the underside of the mushroom, the cap, the stem, the worm's head, and the butterfly. Cut out the trace-offs and use them for pattern pieces. Pin the pieces onto the materials to be used for them and trace around the edges of each. Cut your material ⅛ inch beyond the traced edges, *except* the piece for the butterfly which should be cut along the traced edge. Turn under to the wrong side the ⅛-inch allowance on all pieces *except* the butterfly. Baste, clipping in around any curves so that they do not pucker when pieces are sewn in place.

Pin each piece in position as shown in the design, placing a small piece of cotton padding under the worm's head. Stitch about 6 inches of the ball fringe in place for the body of the worm.

Whip-stitch all remaining pieces *except* the butterfly in place. Pull out the basting threads. Stitch the butterfly with double strands of yellow embroidery floss and a closely placed open buttonhole stitch. Mark the separation of the butterfly wing with a long stitch in yellow embroidery floss. Pencil in lightly all markings shown on the design. Embroider the underside of the mushroom with an outline stitch and a double strand of brown embroidery floss. Embroider the features on the face with an outline stitch and a single strand of black floss. Using double strands of embroidery floss, embroider the hat brim and trim in brown outline stitch and French knots; the butterfly body in brown loop stitch, the head with a brown French knot, and the antennae with brown outline stitch and French knots. Using 6 strands of embroidery floss, embroider the grass in green long stitches.

Sew ball fringe around the neckline of the dress if desired.

**Tablecloth**

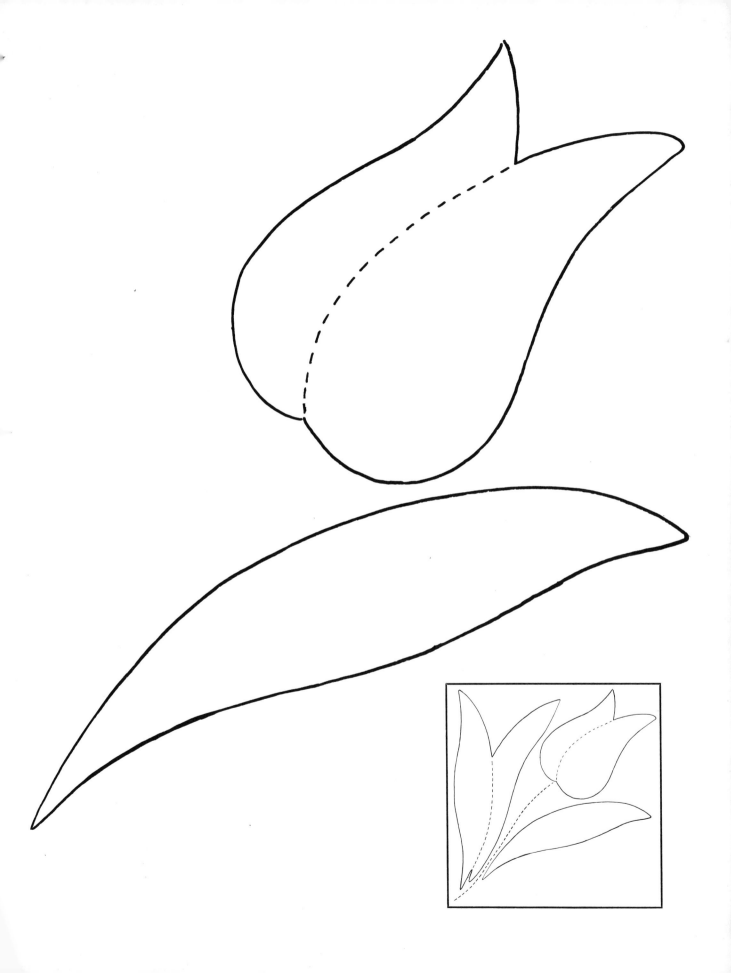

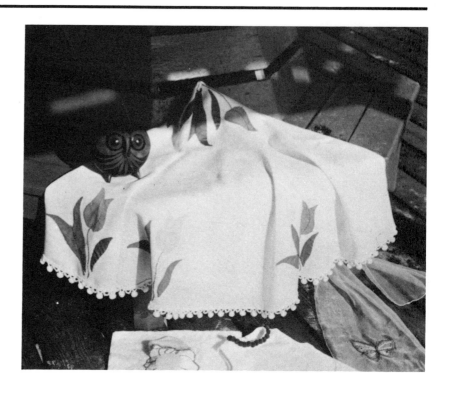

## MATERIALS

72-inch round tablecloth

⅛ yard 36-inch wide orange cotton material for 6 tulips, ⅛ yard of yellow cotton material for 6 more tulips, and ½ yard of green cotton material for leaves

6-strand embroidery floss in green, yellow, and orange

6½ yards of ball fringe for edging around the cloth

Trace off the tulip and leaf motifs, then cut out the trace-offs and use them for pattern pieces. Trace the patterns onto the materials, tracing 6 orange and 6 yellow tulips and 12 single and 12 double green leaves, leaving ½ inch free between each trace-off. Cut your material ⅛ inch beyond the traced edge. Turn under to the wrong side the ⅛-inch allowance and baste, clipping in around any curves so that they do not pucker when pieces are sewn in place.

Fold tablecloth in half and mark along fold with basting thread. Refold again in half in the opposite way and mark in the same manner. Forming a circle, center and pin double leaves along each fold, having bottom point about ½ inch from center point of cloth, then pin tulips (alternating colors) and other leaves in place as shown. Whip-stitch all pieces in place. Pencil in lightly the markings of the dotted lines on the tulips, leaves, and stems. Embroider over them with an outline stitch and self-color floss, working the stems in green and having them meet at the center point of the tablecloth.

Pin four yellow motifs in place at the bottom of the fold lines, centering the tulips on the lines and placing the leaves in position on either side of them, having the bottom point of each double leaf ½ inch up from the edge of the cloth. Whip-stitch these pieces in place and embroider them in the same manner as the center design. Pull out basting threads. Place remaining orange tulip motifs equidistant between these motifs just completed and whip-stitch these in place.

Trim the edge of the tablecloth with ball fringe as shown.

# 2

# *Crewel Embroidery*

Crewel embroidery is a beautiful art form that is used purely for embellishment and ornamentation rather than serving the more functional purposes of some of the other crafts. There is and has always been a need and desire for beauty in the world, so it is not at all surprising that there is evidence that this type of decorative work was done in very ancient times when people's hands were certainly busy enough with the more essential work of weaving goods for their clothing and knotting fibers for their fishnets. Archeological finds in Egypt show horses, warriors, birds and flowers embroidered on ancient tapestries.

Many people find this type of handwork exciting and a particularly interesting outlet for their creative energies. Finished pieces have often been referred to as paintings worked with yarn and a needle. A crewel embroidery needle is the basic tool. A very interesting aspect of this kind of work is that one starts it with only the simplest of stitches, and then goes on to enrich these

stitches in various ways, sometimes re-embroidering other stitches over them, and at other times adding just an extra twist or turn to an already existing stitch. The variety of stitches that can be made in this way is absolutely limitless, and once you have had some experience with crewel work, you will find yourself creating stitches which may never have existed before.

The choice of yarn and background material that may be used for crewel embroidery is almost limitless. Your creativeness comes once again to the fore in your decision whether to work, for example, with six-strand embroidery floss or Persian wool on fine linen or Indianhead, or with knitting worsted or rug yarn on burlap or monk's cloth. The designs shown were made with Persian wool on linen. Though they are beautiful, they are made with simple stitches and designed in a way that allows you to be completely relaxed while attempting your first piece of crewel embroidery.

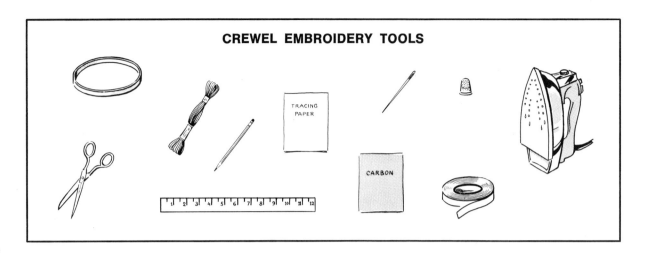

## CREWEL EMBROIDERY TOOLS

## CREWEL EMBROIDERY STITCHES

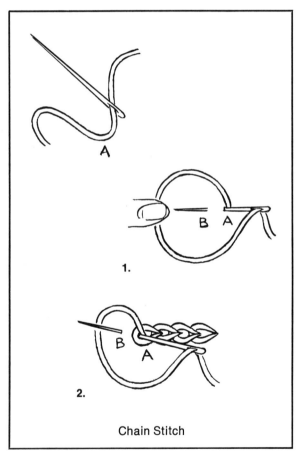

Chain Stitch

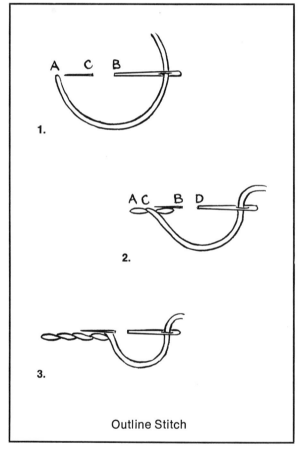

Outline Stitch

Hold work toward you and bring yarn up through traced line, holding yarn down with left thumb. Pass needle through from **A** to **B** (1), pull through. Continue in this manner, passing needle through from **A** to **B** (2).

Bring yarn through at **A** on traced line, pass needle through fabric from **B** to **C** (1), then pass needle through fabric from **D** to **B** (2). Continue working in this manner to completion of stitch (3).

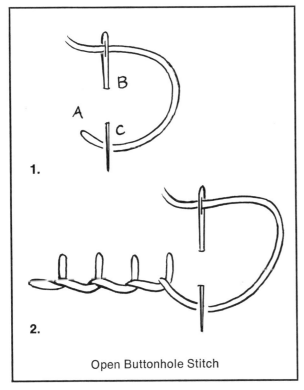

**Open Buttonhole Stitch**

Bring yarn through at **A** on traced line, pass needle through fabric from **B** to **C** (1). Continue working in this manner along traced line to completion of stitch (2).

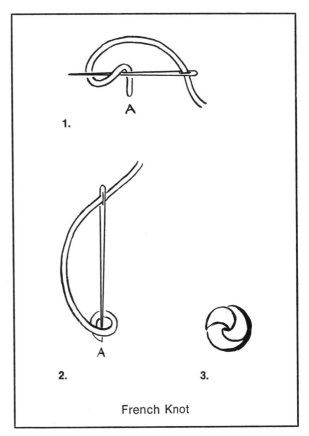

**French Knot**

Bring yarn through at dot on **A,** wrap yarn around needle once (as shown) or as many times as desired (1), then pass needle down through fabric at point **A** (2). Completed stitch looks as shown (3).

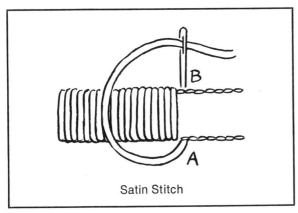

**Satin Stitch**

Bring yarn through at **A** on traced line, then pass needle down through fabric at same place on opposite traced line at **B.** Carry needle across back of material, pass through fabric at point next to **A** and continue to work in same manner as first stitch.

**Long and Short Stitch**

This is a variation of the satin stitch, worked with stitches in irregular rather than regular lengths. On the first row, long and short stitches are alternated along the outline; on following rows, long and short stitches are worked to even the texture.

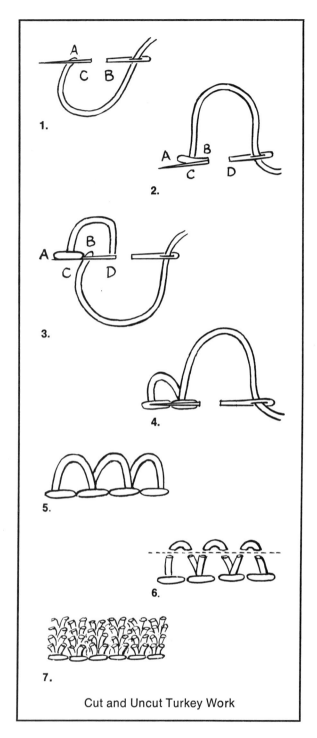

**Cut and Uncut Turkey Work**

stitch, then another loop stitch (4). Continue in this manner to alternate one straight stitch and one loop stitch (5) for uncut turkey work. For cut turkey work, cut (6) and have completed stitch look as shown (7).

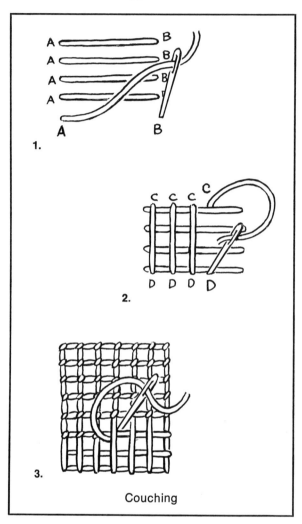

**Couching**

Bring yarn through at **A** on traced line. Pass needle from **B** to **C** (1) and make a straight stitch, then pass needle through fabric from **D** to **B** (2) and leave a loop. Pass needle through fabric from point beyond **D** to **D** (3) and make a straight

Bring yarn through fabric at **A**, carry across traced line to **B** and pass through, then bring yarn through at **B** on next line and carry across to **A**, pass through, and bring up at **A** on next line. Continue in this manner until all horizontal lines are completed (1). Bring yarn through at **C** and continue to work vertical lines in same manner as horizontal lines working from **C** to **D**, **D** to **C**, and so on (2). To finish couching stitch, work a small diagonal stitch across each crossing of vertical and horizontal lines (3).

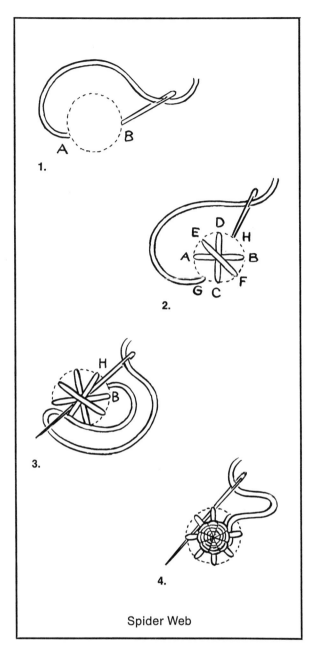

**Spider Web**

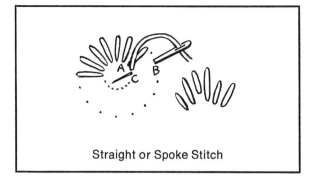

**Straight or Spoke Stitch**

Bring yarn through at **A** on traced line, pass needle through fabric at **B** and bring out at **C**. Continue to work around in this manner.

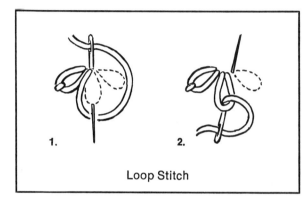

**Loop Stitch**

Bring yarn through at bottom of petal on traced line, then loop yarn and pass needle back through fabric, bringing it up at center top of petal with yarn under needle (1). Make a small stitch over the loop and pass needle through fabric, bringing it up at bottom of next petal (2).

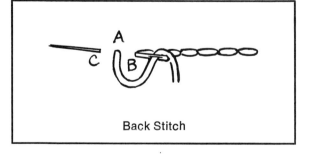

**Back Stitch**

Bring yarn through at **A** on traced line and carry across circle to **B**. Pass needle through fabric at **B** as shown in (1), then continue to work from **C** to **D**, **E** to **F**, and **G** to **H** (2). Bring yarn through at **B** and carry across circle going under spokes and coming out between **A** and **G** (3). Working over **G**, under **C**, over **F**, and under **B**, continue to weave around in this manner until depth of web is completed (4), being sure to work over one spoke and under the next.

This stitch is worked from right to left along traced line. Bring yarn up through traced line at **A**, pass through fabric at **B**, and bring out at **C**. Continue to work in this manner.

## GENERAL INSTRUCTIONS

To make your crewel work easier, it is important that you have all your working materials assembled before you begin your project.

The first step is to cut your material as instructed in your directions. Seal the edges of the cut material by folding masking tape over them to prevent them from fraying while you work.

Next trace off the pattern that you want to work and transfer it onto your material. This should be carefully done; a little patience at this time will assure you of a smoother design to work with. To transfer your design to your material, place dressmaker's carbon on the right side of the fabric with the traced design on top of the carbon, then trace over the design with a pencil. Be careful to hold the design in place, but hold it lightly so that there will be no smudge on your material.

Set your design into embroidery hoops to hold the fabric taut as you work. The size of the frame should be about the size of the area to be embroidered. To use the hoops properly, place your fabric over the smaller hoop, then place the larger hoop over the fabric and press the hoop into place, thus pulling the fabric flat and tight.

Study the stitches you are going to use and practice them a little to be sure that you know exactly how to work them before you start an actual piece of embroidery. A good knowledge of what you are doing will make you feel much more relaxed and will help you to turn out a finer, fault-free piece of work.

Whatever yarn you are using to embroider with should be cut into pieces no longer than 18 inches. This is a good length to work with, long enough to be comfortable and not long enough so that the yarn will snarl or ravel.

Follow stitch and color directions carefully. When your embroidery is done, press it on the wrong side with a warm iron over a damp cloth before the final finishing of your project.

*Note:* We have used Persian wool for our designs because of its nubby textured effect, splitting it into 1 or 2 strands, or using all 3 strands where necessary. You may prefer to use embroidery floss instead of the Persian wool. If you use embroidery floss, remember that 6-strand floss is equal in thickness to a single strand of Persian wool, and therefore you use it as is wherever a single strand of Persian wool is suggested, double where 2 strands are suggested, and triple where 3 strands are suggested.

# Paneled Table Screen

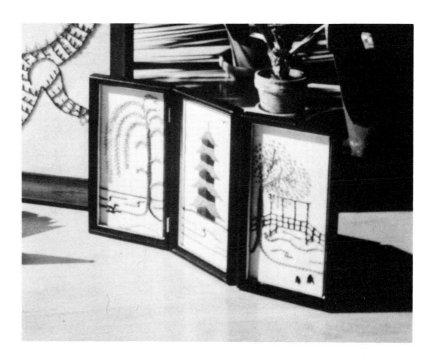

## MATERIALS

4 yards of light blue, and 2 yards each of medium blue, dark blue, and deep blue Persian wool

⅓ yard of 36-inch-wide white linen or Indianhead

3 frames, each with an inside measurement of 7¾ x 3¾ inches

4 small hinges

Measure and mark off on your material 3 panels, each 6 x 10 inches, spaced ½ inch down from the top, ½ inch in from one side edge, and 1 inch apart. Cut your material, allowing for the measured margins. Seal the cut edges. Trace off the 3 different designs you will be using, and transfer them onto your material, centering one on each of the 6 x 10-inch marked-off panels. Set the first panel you will embroider into a hoop. Using a single strand of Persian wool, follow that stitch and color chart to completion. Work your next 2 panels in the same manner, then cut out each 6 x 10-inch panel.

**Finishing:** Press the pieces according to the General Instructions. Frame each one. Attach your center framed panel to each of the end ones, using 2 hinges for each side, and placing them approximately 1½ inches in from the top and bottom of the frames.

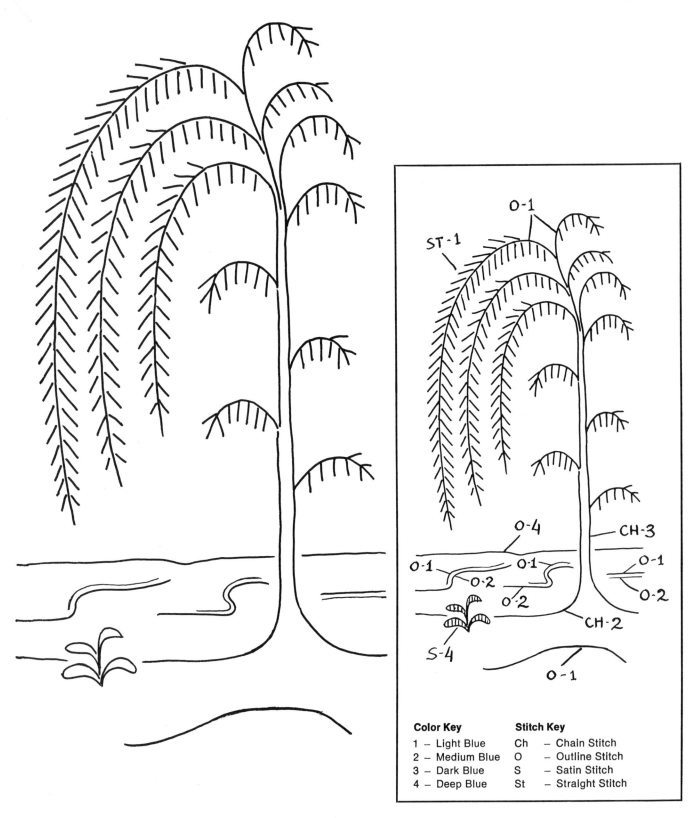

**Color Key**

1 – Light Blue
2 – Medium Blue
3 – Dark Blue
4 – Deep Blue

**Stitch Key**

Ch – Chain Stitch
O – Outline Stitch
S – Satin Stitch
St – Straight Stitch

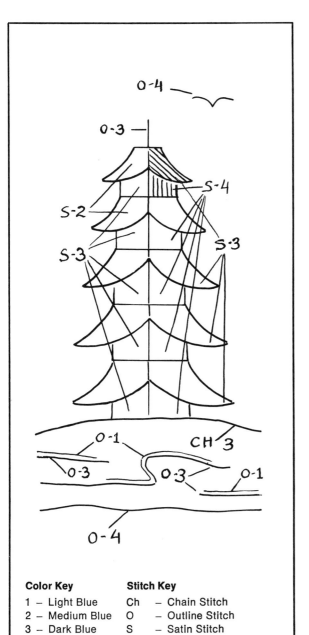

O-4

O-3

S-2

S-4

S-3

S-3

O-1

CH 3

O-3

O-3

O-1

O-4

**Color Key**

1 – Light Blue
2 – Medium Blue
3 – Dark Blue
4 – Deep Blue

**Stitch Key**

Ch – Chain Stitch
O – Outline Stitch
S – Satin Stitch

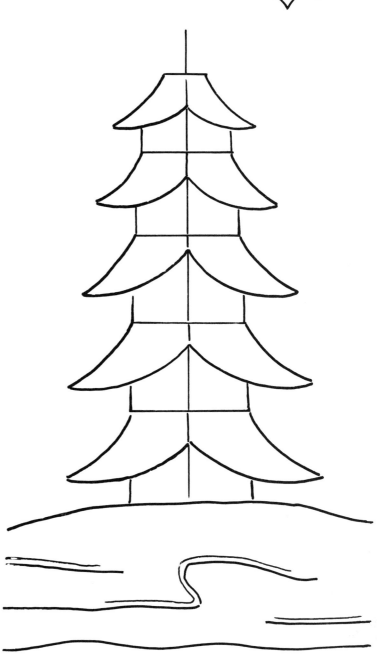

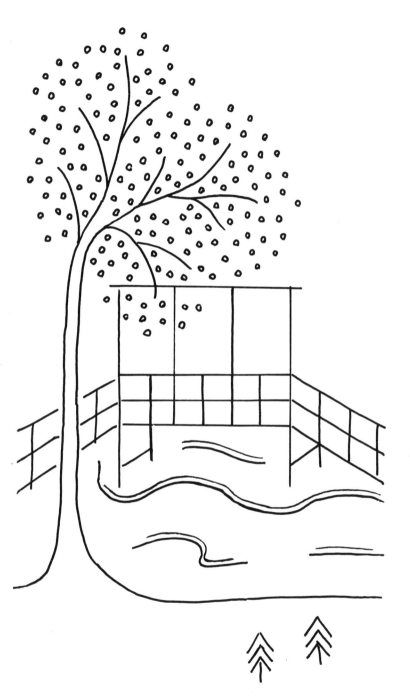

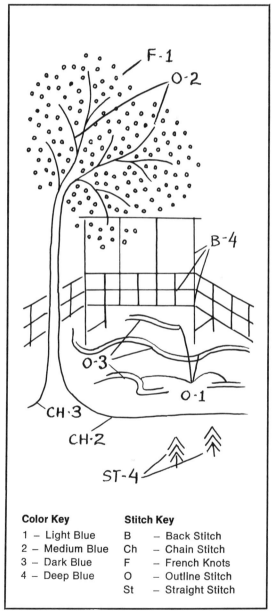

F·1
O·2
B·4
O·3
O·1
CH·3
CH·2
ST·4

**Color Key**
1 — Light Blue
2 — Medium Blue
3 — Dark Blue
4 — Deep Blue

**Stitch Key**
B — Back Stitch
Ch — Chain Stitch
F — French Knots
O — Outline Stitch
St — Straight Stitch

# Book Cover

## MATERIALS

6 yards of light blue, 9 yards each of medium
blue and dark blue, and 15 yards of deep
blue Persian wool
¾ yard of 36-inch-wide white linen or Indianhead
½ yard of soft Pellon for interfacing

Cut your material to the size (when closed) of
the book you are going to cover, allowing 1 inch
additional material at the top and bottom and
at each side edge. Seal the cut edges. Trace your
design, then transfer it onto the center of what
will be the front of the book cover. Transfer 1
flower only from the design onto the center of
what will be the back of the book cover. Set the
portion you will work first into embroidery hoops.
Following the color and stitch chart, start the
design, using 2 strands of Persian wool, and working the flower petals first and the centers last.
Work the other portions of your design in the
same manner.

**Finishing:** Press the cover according to the General Instructions. Cut another piece of material
and a piece of Pellon for interfacing, each to
measure the same size as the embroidered cover.
Cut 2 more pieces, each to measure the height of
the book to be covered, plus an additional 1 x
7¼ inches in width for the inside flaps. Place the
right (exterior) sides of the cover pieces together and the piece for the interfacing on the
wrong side of the embroidered cover piece. Allowing ½ inch for seams, stitch these pieces together
along each long edge. Trim the seams, turn to
right side, and press. Fold each underflap piece
in half lengthwise, with wrong side out. Allowing
½ inch for seams, stitch along each short edge.
Trim, turn right side out, and press. Stitch inside flaps onto the cover with right sides and raw
edges together, allowing ½ inch for seams. Trim
the corners and press seams toward the flaps.
With wrong side out, fold flaps back along cover
and hand-stitch to cover along short ends. Turn
right side out and slip your book into the cover.

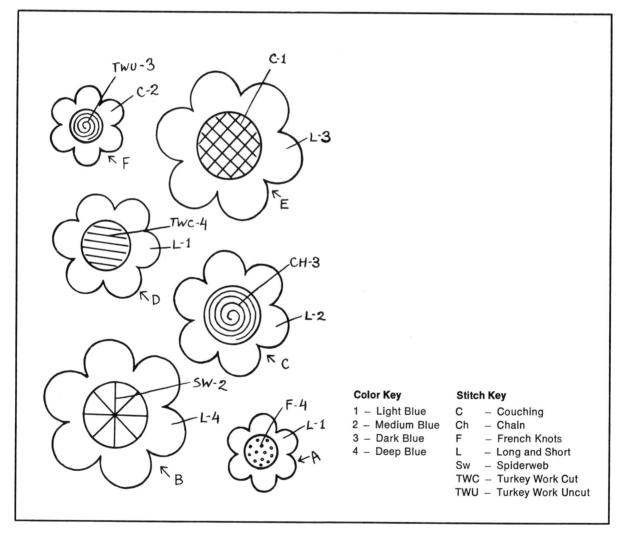

Color Key
1 – Light Blue
2 – Medium Blue
3 – Dark Blue
4 – Deep Blue

Stitch Key
C – Couching
Ch – Chain
F – French Knots
L – Long and Short
Sw – Spiderweb
TWC – Turkey Work Cut
TWU – Turkey Work Uncut

# Dragon Wallhanging

## MATERIALS

15 yards of dark blue Persian wool
15 yards of gold metallic thread
¾ yard of 36-inch-wide white linen or Indianhead
14 x 20-inch frame

Cut your material to measure 23 x 17 inches. Seal the cut edges. Measure off on paper a rectangle 20 inches long and 14 inches wide, then divide your rectangle into 1-inch squares, thus forming a graph 20 boxes long and 14 boxes wide. Following the graph shown, enlarge the design to fit into the boxes you have drawn. Trace off your enlarged design. Centering it, transfer it onto your material. Place hoops on your work and, using 2 strands of Persian wool and one of metallic thread, follow the stitch and color chart to completion.

**Finishing:** Press your piece according to the General Instructions, then frame it.

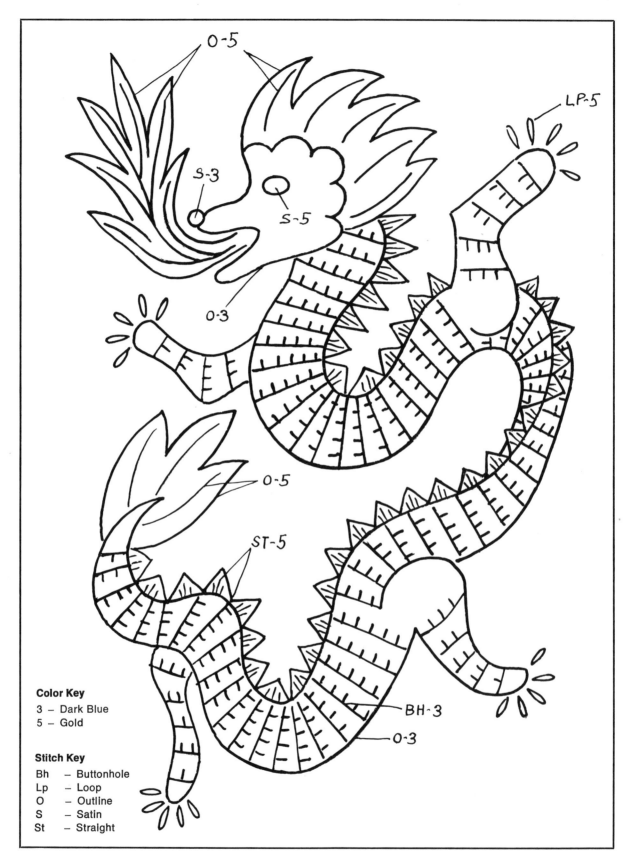

O-5

LP-5

S-3

S-5

O-3

O-5

ST-5

BH-3

O-3

**Color Key**

3 — Dark Blue
5 — Gold

**Stitch Key**

Bh — Buttonhole
Lp — Loop
O — Outline
S — Satin
St — Straight

# 3

# Crocheting

Crocheting is one of the most popular of crafts, and the technique is very easy to learn and to master. Your basic working tool is just a single small needle, hooked at one end, and it is very exciting to see beautiful things develop, row by row, with the use of the little crochet hook, some yarn, and a series of simple, interlocking stitches. In this type of work there are actually only a very few basic stitches to learn, and it is the combining of the various stitches, rather than the stitches themselves, that adds to the beauty and interest of the work.

We have referred to the crochet hook as a small needle, and this is because its length, on the average, is only about 6 inches. Although the length of the shaft generally remains the same, the range of hook sizes is very broad. A crochet hook number designates the actual thickness of the little hook at the end of the shaft. The weight of the yarn you work with on any project determines the size of the hook you will use, and the gradation of the hook sizes is broad enough to encompass any type of yarn from the very finest cotton to the heaviest weight wool.

Throughout the centuries crocheting was used primarily as a way of making beautiful laces, and these were always made with very fine thread and a sliver-thin hook. It is only in comparatively recent times that crocheters realized that the needle could be sized to accommodate many other types of yarn besides very fine thread. With this knowledge there developed quite suddenly a rash of wonderful new ideas and designs for things to crochet. People began to make exciting clothes for themselves and lovely pieces of home decor, and they discovered, as they did it, how quickly

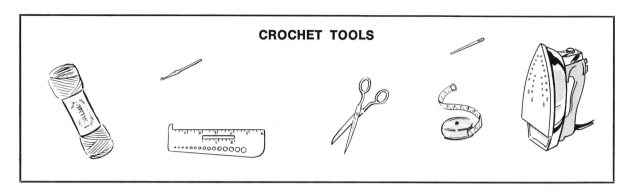

**CROCHET TOOLS**

the work went and how much they enjoyed doing it.

Aside from the fun of working in this new-old art form and the excitement of watching large pieces of interesting texture develop from the little one-by-one stitches, there are other reasons people enjoy this particular type of work so much. Crochet is a simple one-needle craft in which each row and, in fact, each stitch is a finished thing unto itself. When crocheting, you can easily see exactly how your work is coming along at the end of each row.

You may lay down your work at any point without fearing that your stitches will slip off your needle and your work will unravel. When the last stitch you have worked has been completed, no matter where it occurs, there remains only one single loop on your hook. When you choose to stop your work for a while, you need only to withdraw your hook from that one loop, lay your work aside, and then start over again when you are ready.

The number of things that can be made is limitless. Some of the most interesting are those which are made up of several small pieces, each one finished unto itself and then joined together into a much larger piece, such as an afghan or a rug. Many people very much enjoy this particular way of crocheting, for they find the small pieces easy to work on and easy to carry around with them wherever they happen to be, and they like making one little piece after another until finally there are enough to assemble into that total piece they are working toward. This type of work is rather like putting together the pieces of a jigsaw puzzle.

Several interesting designs are offered here in both straight crocheting and in the kind of work composed of the many little pieces (frequently referred to as "granny square" or "patchwork" crochet). We describe what little equipment you need to start with and how to work the various stitches, and then, since there are a few general rules to know before starting to work in this or any other craft medium, we tell you what the rules are for this one. Many happy leisure hours lie ahead for you if you learn how to crochet.

## CROCHET STITCHES

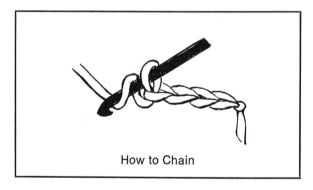

How to Chain

Knot a loop onto hook. Holding hook in your right hand, the end of yarn extending from the loop in your left hand, and the main length of yarn over the index finger of your left hand, * place main length over hook, then draw the yarn and hook through the loop (1st stitch), repeat from * for the desired number of stitches on your foundation chain. Any pattern stitch may be worked on this foundation chain. Turning chains are worked in the same way. Where chain stitches are indicated in a pattern stitch, they are also done in the same way, using the last loop worked as the first one through which your yarn and hook are drawn.

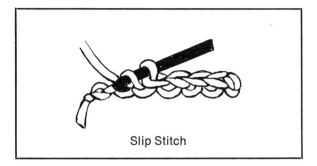

Slip Stitch

Insert hook in stitch, yarn over hook and draw through stitch and through loop on hook.

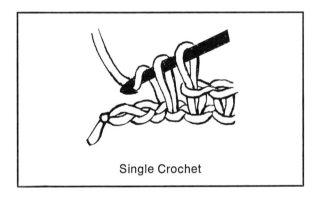

Single Crochet

Insert hook in stitch, yarn over hook and draw through stitch, yarn over and draw through remaining 2 loops on hook.

Half Double Crochet

Yarn over hook, insert hook in stitch, yarn over and draw through the stitch, yarn over and draw through remaining 3 loops on hook.

## GENERAL INSTRUCTIONS

The most important thing to remember in crocheting is that the texture you are making must conform exactly to the texture called for in the pattern you are following. The word **Gauge** appears at the beginning of every set of crochet directions, and it is most essential that you pay attention to it. It tells exactly how loose or tight the texture of your work must be, a factor controlled by the number of stitches you get to every inch of your work. This is determined by the size of the crochet hook you use, the yarn you are working with, and the individual tension in your hands.

A suggested hook size is also given with each set of directions, but it is most important that you experiment on a small piece with the suggested size hook to find out if your own tension, which is a very individual thing, gives you the same number of stitches per inch as those called for in the gauge. If you are getting more stitches to the inch, then you must experiment with a larger hook; if you are getting fewer stitches, then you must try a smaller hook. It is unwise to begin any crochet project before you are sure that you are getting exactly the right tension, for if there is any variation, your finished piece will not come out to the proper size. The best way to test your gauge is to make a 3-inch square with the yarn you are going to use, then measure the number of stitches per inch on your stitch gauge ruler, and make whatever adjustments you feel may be necessary.

A yarn requirement is also given under **Materials** at the beginning of every set of crochet directions. If it is at all possible, you should buy at one time the total amount specified. Sometimes a color does run out, and sometimes a new dye lot varies in shade from the one that you started with. It is dismaying to come halfway through a piece of work only to discover that you cannot get any more of the same color or dye lot to complete your project. If you find that for some reason you cannot buy all the yarn at one time, ask the shopkeeper to lay away for you whatever quantity you will need beyond the amount you are initially buying. Yarn dealers understand the necessity for having all your yarn in the same color and dye lot, and are quite willing to cooperate.

Included in the crochet patterns is a child's pants tunic, with a coordinated cap and scarf. Directions for the tunic are written for sizes 4 through 12, and for the cap and scarf for sizes small (4 to 6 years old), medium (8 to 10 years old) and large (12 years old). In crocheting, the desired size for a sweater, dress, or tunic is determined by the bust or chest measurement. Children's standard size measurements 4 through 12 are given in the table. Carefully measure the chest size of the child for whom you are going to make the tunic, then compare the number of inches you get to those given on the chart for the various sizes. The one which comes closest to your measurement is the right one for the child.

**Suggested Standard Size Measurements**

| Children's sizes | 4 | 6 | 8 | 10 | 12 |
|---|---|---|---|---|---|
| Chest measurement | 23″ | 24″ | 26″ | 28″ | 30″ |

Read the directions very carefully, *step by step* as you work. Read only the first thing you need to know and do that for the necessary number of inches or rows indicated, then go on to read what needs to be done next. You will find this an easy way to work, and you will not become confused by figures and directions which are of no value at all until you reach the point in your work where you need to know what to do next.

When you have completed the first skein of yarn you are working with and need to start on another, **join the new ball only at the end of a row,** even though this may mean that you will need to cut away and waste a small length of yarn. By joining at the end only, your work will have a much neater finish.

When an *asterisk* (*) appears in a set of directions, it indicates that the instructions immediately following it are to be repeated the additional number of times specified.

When a portion of any set of directions is set within *parentheses* ( ), those instructions within the parentheses must be repeated in the exact order they are given for the number of time indicated by the numeral immediately following the close of the parentheses. This has to be done before going on to the remaining instructions for the completion of the pattern row in which they appear.

When **changing colors** in your work, the last stitch of the original color is worked with that color to the point where 2 loops of that last stitch remain on the hook and then those 2 loops are removed with the new color. Colors are indicated in directions as MC for Main Color, CC for Contrast Color, A for Color A, B for Color B, and so on for as many colors as are used in any design.

When an **increase** in your work is indicated, you do this by working 2 stitches in the same stitch where the increase is to occur. This is generally done by making the extra stitch in the same pattern as the original one in which the increase is being made.

When it is necessary to **decrease** in your work, you do this by working off 2 stitches as 1, thus decreasing or "losing" 1 stitch whenever this is done. As an example of how to decrease in single crochet work, you would insert your needle into the next stitch to be worked, place your yarn over the hook, draw through the stitch, insert the needle into the next stitch, place yarn over hook again, draw through that stitch, then yarn over hook once more and draw through all remaining loops.

When a **pompon** is called for in your design, make this by winding yarn around two or more fingers (depending on the desired diameter) approximately between 25 and 50 times, depending on the thickness desired, then remove the yarn from your fingers and tie securely through the center, leaving a short end with which to attach the pompon. Clip the end loops and trim them evenly.

Where **fringe** is called for, make this by cutting several strands of yarn each to measure 1 inch longer than double the desired length, then fold the stands in half, draw the loop formed through the number of stitches indicated, draw the loose ends through the loop, and draw taut.

**Seaming** is necessary in practically whatever you make, other than straight flat pieces, such as the child's scarf designed for this chapter. The simplest and best way to make your seams is with the use of a blunt-edge tapestry needle and a ½-inch running back stitch on the wrong side of your work.

Every finished garment should be **blocked,** and this can be done either before or after the pieces have been seamed together. Blocking should be done with a warm iron over a damp cloth placed on the work. Avoid pressing hard or holding the iron too long in any one place.

*Note:* Some of the patterns have been designed with granny squares. Though the effects are different, the squares are always made in the same way. For this reason the directions for the square are given first, and we will refer you as necessary to those directions in the making of each of the different designs.

# Granny Square

*Each finished square measures 4¾ inches.*

## MATERIALS

Small amounts each of melon (Main Color), orange (Color A), olive (Color B), and gold (Color C), of knitting worsted. The actual amount for each design will be specified in the directions for it.

No. G aluminum crochet hook

**Gauge:** 4 stitches = 1 inch.

With MC, chain 4, join to form a ring.

**Round 1:** Chain 2, work 3 single crochet in center of ring, * chain 2, 4 single crochet in center of ring, repeat from * twice and end with a slip stitch in the top of the starting chain 2. Fasten off.

**Round 2:** Attach A to any chain-2 corner space, chain 2 and work 1 single crochet in same space, * chain 2, skip 4 single crochet, work 2 single crochet, chain 2 and 2 single crochet in the next space, repeat from * twice more and end with chain 2, skip 4 single crochet, 2 single crochet in same space as 1st chain-2, chain 2 and end with a slip stitch in the top of the starting chain-2. Fasten off.

**Round 3:** Attach MC to any chain-2 corner space, chain 2, work 1 single crochet in same space, * chain 2, skip 2 single crochet, work 3 single crochet in next space, chain 2, work 2 single crochet, chain 2 and 2 single crochet in corner space, repeat from * twice more and end with chain 2, skip 2 single crochet, 3 single crochet in next space, chain 2, 2 single crochet in same space as 1st chain-2, chain 2 and end with a slip stitch in the top of the starting chain-2. Fasten off.

**Round 4:** Attach B to any chain-2 corner space, chain 2, work 1 single crochet in same space, * work 3 single crochet in each of the next 2 chain-2 spaces, 2 single crochet, chain 2 and 2 single crochet in the corner space, repeat from * twice more and end with 3 single crochet in each of the next 2 chain-2 spaces, 2 single crochet in same space as 1st chain-2, chain 2 and end with a slip stitch in the top of the starting chain-2. Fasten off.

**Round 5:** Attach MC to any chain-2 corner space, chain 2, work 2 single crochet in the same space, * work 1 single crochet in each single crochet to the next chain-2 corner space, 3 single crochet in that space, repeat from * 3 times more and end with a slip stitch in the top of the starting chain-2. Fasten off.

**Round 6:** Attach C to any corner stitch, chain 2, work 2 half double crochet in the same stitch, * work 1 half double crochet in each single crochet to the next corner stitch, work 3 half double crochet in that stitch, repeat from * 3 times more and end with a slip stitch in the top of the starting chain-2. Fasten off.

**Round 7:** Attach MC to any corner stitch, chain 2, work 2 single crochet in the same stitch, * work 1 single crochet in each half double crochet to the next corner stitch, work 3 single crochet in that stitch, repeat from * 3 times more and end with a slip stitch in the top of the starting chain-2. Fasten off.

**Round 8:** Attach B to any corner stitch and repeat Round 6.

# Cap and Scarf Set

*Directions are written for small size (4 to 6 years old). Changes for medium size (8 to 10 years old) and large size (12 years old) are in parentheses.*

## MATERIALS

1 4-ounce skein each of melon (Main Color) and olive (Contrast Color) and 1 2-ounce skein each of orange (Color A) and gold (Color B) of knitting worsted for both pieces and all sizes

No. G and No. J aluminum crochet hooks

**Gauge:** 7 stitches on No. J hook = 2 inches.

# Cap

**Ribbing:** With CC and No. G hook, chain 7 stitches. **Row 1:** Single crochet in 2nd chain from hook and in each chain across row, chain 1, turn. Working in single crochet now through back loops of the stitches only, work even on 6 stitches until piece measures 13 (15, 16) inches. Fasten off.

**Crown: Row 1:** Attach MC to point where CC was just fastened off, and working with a No. J hook, work 65 (72, 76) single crochet along the top long edge of the ribbing strip. Fasten off MC. Working on these stitches now, and working all MC rows in single crochet and all other color rows in half double crochet and increasing 7 (6, 8) stitches evenly spaced on Row 5, work in color pattern as follows, working the small size through Row 13 only:

**Row 2: B. Row 3: MC. Row 4: A. Row 5: MC. Row 6: CC. Rows 7, 8, 9, 10 and 11: MC. Rows 12, 13, 14, 15, 16, and 17:** Repeat Rows 6, 5, 4, 3, 2, and 1. When striped portion has been completed, work in CC only and working the 1st row in half double crochet and the remaining rows in single crochet, **Shape Top** as follows: **Row 1:** Work even on 72 (78, 84) stitches. **Row 2:** * Work across 10 (11, 12) stitches, decrease 1 stitch, repeat from * across row—6 decreases have been made and 66 (72, 78) stitches remain. **Row 3:** * Work across 9 (10, 11) stitches, decrease 1 stitch,

repeat from * across row—60 (66, 72) stitches remain. **Row 4:** * Work across 8 (9, 10) stitches, decrease 1 stitch, repeat from * across row—54 (60, 66) stitches remain. Continue in this manner to decrease 6 stitches evenly spaced on each row, having 1 stitch less between each point of decrease until 36 (42, 48) stitches remain. **Next Row:** Work 2 stitches together across row—18 (21, 24) stitches remain. **Next Row:** * Work 1 stitch, decrease 1 stitch, repeat from * across row—12 (14, 16) stitches remain. **Next Row:** Work 2 stitches together now—6 (7, 8) stitches remain. Fasten off yarn, leaving a long thread.

**Finishing:** Draw thread tightly through remaining stitches and sew the back seam. Press cap flat, folding the bottom portion under and pressing along the center of the broad MC stripe. Make a CC pompon of desired size and sew to the top of the cap.

# Scarf

With CC and No. J hook, chain 75 (89, 89) stitches. **Row 1:** Single crochet in 2nd chain from hook and in each chain across row, chain 1, turn. Working even on 74 (88, 88) stitches and working MC rows in single crochet and all other color rows in half double crochet, work 1 row with CC then repeat Rows 1 through 11 as on the cap. On the large size only, work 2 additional rows of MC after Row 11, then on all sizes repeat Rows 12 through 17. When this striped portion has been completed, work 1 more row of CC half double crochet, and 1 row of CC slip stitch. Fasten off.

**Finishing:** With CC, work 1 row of single crochet along each of the short ends of the scarf. **Fringe:** Cut several strands of CC fringe, each to measure 9 inches. Knot 4 strands in every other stitch along these short ends. Trim fringe ends evenly. Block.

# Child's Pants Tunic

*Directions are written for size 4. Changes for sizes 6, 8, 10, and 12 are in parentheses.*

## MATERIALS

2 (2, 2, 3, 3) 4-ounce skeins melon (Main Color) and 1 4-ounce skein olive (Contrast Color), and a small amount of orange (Color A), and gold (Color B) of knitting worsted for all sizes

No. G and No. J aluminum crochet hooks

**Gauge:** 7 stitches on No. J hook = 2 inches.

**Back:** With MC and No. J hook, chain 52 (54, 57, 61, 65) stitches.

**Row 1:** Single crochet in 2nd chain from hook and in each chain across row, chain 1, turn. Working in single crochet throughout, work even now on 51 (53, 56, 60, 64) stitches for 2 inches, then decrease 1 stitch at the beginning and end of the next row and repeat this decrease every 1½ (1½, 2, 2, 2½) inches 4 times more. Work even now on 41 (43, 46, 50, 54) stitches until piece measures 12½ (13, 13½, 14, 14½) inches or 2 inches less than desired length to underarm, ending with a wrong-side row. **Shape Armholes:** Slip stitch across 3 (3, 3, 4, 4) stitches, work to within last 3 (3, 3, 4, 4) stitches, chain and turn. Work 1 row even, then decrease 1 stitch at the beginning and end of the next row. Work even now on 33 (35, 38, 40, 44) stitches until piece measures 1 inch above the start of the armhole shaping, ending

with a wrong-side row. **Shape Neck:** Work across 14 (15, 16, 17, 18) stitches, chain and turn. Decrease 1 stitch at the beginning of the next row and repeat this decrease every other row 4 times more. Work even now on 9 (10, 11, 12, 13) stitches until piece measures 4½ (5, 5½, 6, 6½) inches above the start of the armhole shaping, ending with a wrong-side row. **Shape Shoulders:** Slip stitch across 5 (5, 6, 6, 7) stitches, work to end of row, chain and turn. **Next Row:** Slip stitch across remaining 4 (5, 5, 6, 6) stitches. Fasten off. Return to row where neck shaping began, skip center 5 (5, 6, 6, 8) stitches, attach yarn to next stitch and work 2nd half of top to correspond to 1st half.

**Front:** Work in same manner as for back.

**Finishing:** Sew side and shoulder seams. **Pocket:** Make 1 granny square and sew it onto the front of the tunic, sewing along the bottom and two sides only, and placing it approximately 2½ inches up from the bottom and 1 inch in from the side seam of the tunic. With MC, work 1 row single crochet around the neck and armhole edges, then with CC work 1 row single crochet around these same edges. **Fringe:** Cut several strands of CC, each to measure 4 inches. Knot 3 strands in every other stitch around the neck edge, and 4 in every other stitch around the bottom. Trim fringe ends evenly. Block.

# Slipper Scuffs

*Directions are written for small size (2 to 4 years old). Changes for medium size (6 to 8 years old) and large sizes 12, 14, 16, 18, and 20 are in parentheses.*

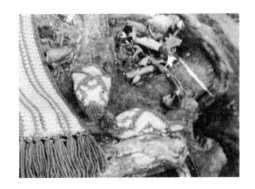

### MATERIALS

2 (2, 4) ounces melon (Main Color) and 1 ounce each of olive (Contrast Color), orange (Color A), and gold (Color B) of knitting worsted for all sizes

No. G aluminum crochet hook (for small size), No. I (for medium size), and No. K (for large size).

Using the proper size hook for the desired size slippers, make 2 granny squares, one for the sole of each slipper and 2 granny squares through Round

4 only for each of the toe portions.

**To Finish Each Slipper:** Fold the complete square in half, opposite points to each other, and tack these points together. Fit one of the smaller front portion squares into the larger folded one, placing one point of the smaller square to the tacked portion, the opposite point of the smaller one to the opposite point of the joined points of the large square, and the two side points of the smaller square overlapping on each side. Sew in place. Trim the point of each slipper with a small CC pompon.

# Fringed Pillow

## MATERIALS

3 4-ounce skeins of olive knitting worsted
No. J aluminum crochet hook
14-inch pillow form
½ yard of 36-inch-wide material

**Gauge:** 7 stitches on No. J hook = 2 inches.

Chain 49 stitches. **Row 1:** Single crochet in 2nd chain from hook and in each chain across row, chain 1, turn. Working in single crochet throughout, work even on 48 stitches until piece measures 14 inches. Fasten off.

**Fringe:** Cut several strands of yarn, each to measure 4½ inches. Knotting fringe along every 4th row, knot 3 strands for fringe in the following order: * fringe in each of the 1st 2 stitches, skip the next stitch, repeat from * across row. Trim ends evenly.

**Tassels:** Make 4: Cut 25 strands of yarn, each to measure 8½ inches. Fold the strands in half and tie them together at the center. Fold them in half at the center point, cut another strand of yarn and tie this tightly around the tassel, approximately 1 inch down from the center tie. Trim ends evenly.

**Finishing:** Cut material to measure the size of the fringed crochet piece. Sew two pieces together along 3 sides, insert the pillow form, then sew the 4th side. Sew one tassel on each corner.

# Afghan

*Approximate size with fringe 54 x 63 inches.*

## MATERIALS

6 4-ounce skeins each of melon (Main Color) and olive (Contrast Color) and 1 skein each of orange (Color A), and gold (Color B) knitting worsted
No. G and No. J aluminum crochet hooks

**Gauge:** 7 stitches on No. J hook = 2 inches.

**Strip A** (make 6): With No. G hook, make 54 granny squares. Make the 6 strips by sewing 9 squares together for each one, joining one square to the other by sewing them along 1 edge only.

**Strip B** (make 2): With MC and No. J hook, chain 136 stitches.

**Row 1:** Single crochet in 2nd chain from hook and in each chain across row, chain 1, turn. Working even on 135 stitches, and working the MC rows in single crochet and all other color rows in half double crochet, work in color pattern as follows: **Row 2: B. Row 3: MC. Row 4: A. Row 5: MC. Row 6: CC. Rows 7, 8, 9, 10, and 11: MC. Rows 12, 13, 14, 15, and 16:** Repeat Rows 6, 5, 4, 3 and 2, then work 1 more row with MC. Fasten off.

**Strip C:** Make 1: With MC and No. J hook, chain 136 stitches. Single crochet in 2nd chain from hook and in each chain across row, chain 1, turn. Working in single crochet throughout, work even on 135 stitches until piece measures 14 inches. Fasten off.

**Finishing:** With No. J hook and CC work 1 row of single crochet around the 4 sides of Strips B and C, working 135 stitches along each long edge of each strip and as many stitches as necessary along each short edge to make the work lie flat, and working 3 single crochet in each corner stitch as you turn. Work in same manner around the A strips, working 4 of these strips on the 2 long sides only, and working the remaining 2 (top and bottom strips) along 1 long and 2 short sides only. Arrange strips according to chart below, and sew them together, joining the top and bottom A strips to the rest of the afghan along those side edges which do not have the final row of MC single crochet. **Fringe:** Cut several strands of CC, each to measure 10 inches and knot 3 strands in every other stitch along the 4 sides of the afghan. Trim fringe ends evenly. Block.

**Chart for Arrangement of Afghan Strips**

| | | | | | | | |
|---|---|---|---|---|---|---|---|
| STRIP A | | | | | | | |
| S T R I P A | S T R I P B | S T R I P A | STRIP C | S T R I P A | S T R I P B | S T R I P A | |
| STRIP A | | | | | | | |

# Knitting

Knitting is a very interesting two-needle craft which offers pleasurable recreation to people of all ages. It is easy to learn how to knit and fascinating to discover what wonderful things you can make with your two hands, some yarn, a pair of needles, and the simple knit and purl stitches. There is something very relaxing and soothing about the steady rhythmic clicking of a pair of needles involved with a ball of yarn toward the ultimate creation of a thing of your very own. This may be either something to wear or to use as a part of your home decor, or perhaps a most welcome gift to a newborn baby, a friend who loves to ski, or a neighbor who would enjoy the cuddly warmth of a handmade knitted shawl or sweater.

To start on any knitting project, you will need a few simple tools to work with. To become a good knitter, you should observe the basic and very important General Instructions which appear in this chapter just before the directions given for making the special things we have designed for you. Take a little extra time to study these elementary guides and remember them well as you start out on your first real knitting project. By having learned them, your work will be good, and you will be the first to enjoy and be proud of your new skill. Observance of the gauge, for example, will make the difference between the good-fitting knitted design that you want to make and the beautiful little "bird" sweaters and the 10-foot-long scarves too often found at bazaar counters, the results of some well-intentioned labor of love on the part of a knitter who has chosen to ignore the gauge, or the number of stitches one is getting to an inch.

A myriad of colors and weights and types of

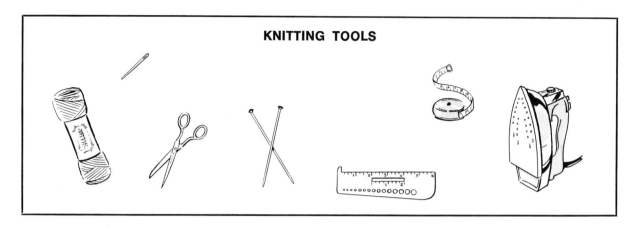

## KNITTING TOOLS

yarn are available, and just to look at the selection in a good store is temptation enough to make you want to start knitting. You may want to make a high-fashion vest or skirt like the ones that are so in style these days, or perhaps the lovely handknit basic sweater that you've always wanted to own. Do be tempted, and once you have started making some of our lovely things, you will be glad for the little spare time you take now to learn how to be a good knitter.

## KNITTING STITCHES

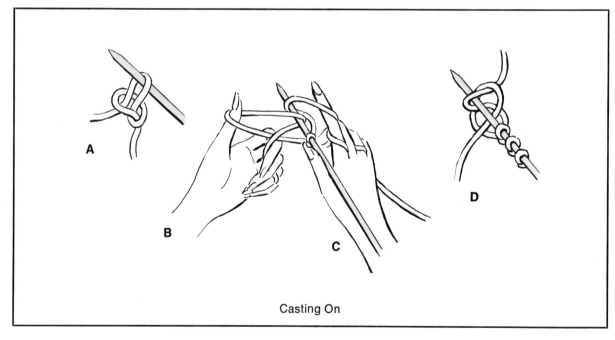

Casting On

Make a loop on needle, allowing a 2-yard end of yarn for every 100 stitches that need to be cast on, more if your yarn is a heavier than average weight and less if it is lighter. This is your first stitch, **A.** Hold needle in your right hand with short end of yarn toward you, then * (1) with short end make a loop on left thumb and insert needle from front to back through this loop, **B;** (2) place yarn attached to ball under and around needle, **C;** (3) draw yarn through loop and pull short end down to tighten it, **D;** (4) repeat from * for desired number of stitches.

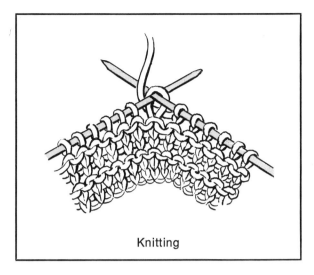

Knitting

Holding needle with cast-on stitches in your left hand with yarn to back of work, * insert right needle from left to right through front of first stitch, wrap yarn completely around right needle forming a loop, slip needle and loop through stitch to front, and slip stitch just worked off left needle. This is your first stitch. Repeat from * in same manner across all stitches on left needle.

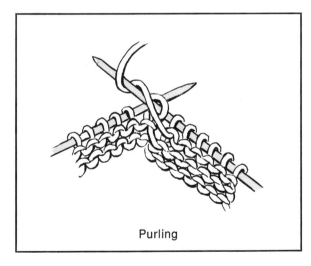

Purling

* Holding yarn in front of work, insert right needle from right to left through front of first stitch on left needle, wrap yarn completely around right needle, forming a loop, slip needle and loop through stitch to back and slip stitch just worked off left needle. Repeat from * until all stitches are worked.

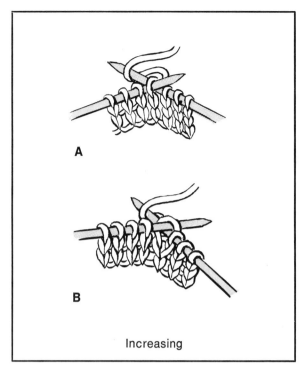

A

B

Increasing

Insert right needle from right to left through back of next stitch on left needle, wrap yarn completely around needle, forming a loop, **A,** and slip needle and loop through to front, forming a new stitch on right needle, then knit the same stitch on left needle in usual manner, **B,** and slip the stitch from left needle.

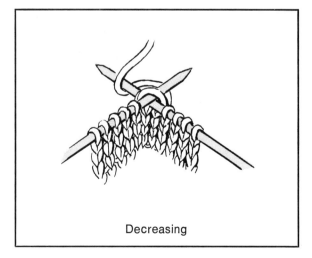

Decreasing

Insert right needle through 2 stitches on left needle and work these stitches together as **one** stitch.

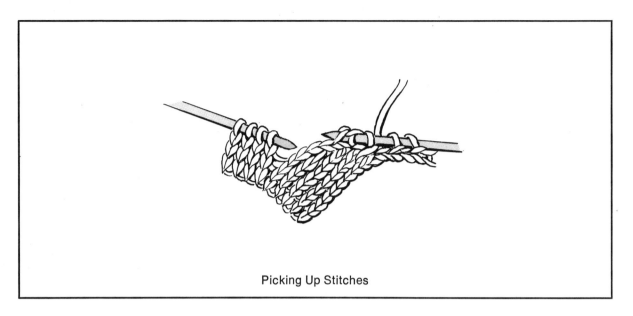

Picking Up Stitches

Picking up stitches, as is necessary around a neck or an armhole, is always done on the right side of work, and usually started at a seam edge, such as the top of one shoulder for neck stitches, or at the underarm for an armhole shaping. Stitches are picked up by inserting your right needle through the center of the desired stitch and knitting that stitch in the usual manner onto your right needle, fitting the number of stitches evenly into the complete space available for picking up stitches.

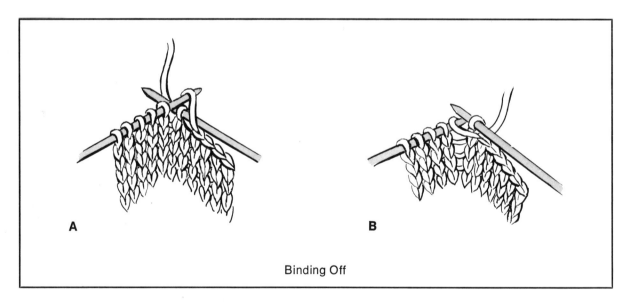

A          B

Binding Off

Knit first 2 stitches, then * insert point of left needle into the 1st stitch on right needle, **A,** and lift this stitch over the 2nd stitch and drop off needle, **B.** Knit another stitch and repeat from * across for necessary number of stitches to be bound off. When all stitches are to be bound off at the end of a piece of work, and when one stitch remains, break off the yarn and fasten off by drawing remaining yarn through that last stitch.

Appliqué, the art of cutouts

Decorating with crewel embroidery

Samples of the versatile art of knitting

Color and crochet

Latchet hooking—especially good for rugs

Objects in macramé, the art of knotting

Variety in needlepoint and bargello

Fun with patchwork designs

## GENERAL INSTRUCTIONS

In any set of knitting directions, you will find a yarn requirement, a suggested needle size, and a stitch measurement guide or gauge. To start knitting, you will first need yarn, and your only concern in buying whichever yarn you choose is to purchase a sufficient amount of the particular color you are going to work with to be able to complete the garment you are planning to make. Dye lots vary, and you could spoil the perfection of your work if it became necessary for you to use two different lots. Most yarn shopkeepers are aware of this problem, and they are quite willing to lay away spare yarn for you if you do not want to buy the entire amount at one time, or to accept for refund whatever full skeins you may have bought in excess of the amount you actually use.

In most knitting directions, including our own, there appears along with the yarn requirement a suggested needle size. The size given is the one used by the average knitter to achieve the correct gauge with the yarn that is recommended. It is very important to know, however, that there is the possibility of a great amount of variation in the tension of the individual hand and that you yourself may not come at all close with the suggested needles and yarn to the gauge you must achieve.

**Gauge** is the key word that spells out the final success or failure of any project. In knitting it means the number of stitches you are getting to an inch. To be a good knitter you should swatch out a 3-inch square with the yarn you are going to use and the suggested size needles. You should then measure your swatch on your stitch gauge ruler to determine if you are getting the same number of stitches per inch as that called for in the pattern you are working with. If you are getting more than the prescribed number, try larger needles; if you are getting fewer, then make another sample piece using smaller needles. When you have gotten the exact number of stitches called for, then you will know what needles to use and you will be sure that whatever you make will come out to the proper size.

In our patterns, the cap has been designed to fit an average 20- to 22-inch adult head size. The woman's slipover and vest can be made in any size from 10 to 20, and the man's sleeveless cardigan can be made in small (36–38), medium (40–42), and large (44–46) sizes. Chest or bust measurement determines the correct size. Measure yourself or the person for whom you are going to make the sweater, then compare that measurement with the various sizes shown in the chart. You will then know which size comes closest to the one that you want to make.

**Suggested Standard Size Measurements**

| Women's sizes | 10 | 12 | 14 | 16 | 18 | 20 |
|---|---|---|---|---|---|---|
| Bust measurement | 32″ | 34″ | 36″ | 38″ | 40″ | 42″ |

| Men's sizes | Small (36–38) | Medium (40–42) | Large (44–46) |
|---|---|---|---|
| Chest measurement | 37″ | 41″ | 45″ |

When reading your directions, *read them step by step* and follow them as you read. It is confusing to read an entire set of directions at one time.

When it is necessary to **join another ball of yarn,** do so only at the beginning or end of a row. This will give a neater appearance to your work.

When **ribbing** is called for in any design, this is done by alternating 1 knit and 1 purl stitch across the first row, and then knitting the purl stitches and purling the knit stitches of the previous row on all following rows. Ribbing is usually worked on needles two to three sizes smaller than those used for proper gauge.

**Seams** are joined with the same yarn with which the pieces were made, and those pieces should be carefully matched and pinned before they are joined. There are a few methods of seaming, but the one we prefer is done with a blunt-edge tapestry needle and the use of a ½-inch running back stitch on the wrong side of the work.

**Blocking** should be done with a warm iron over a damp cloth. Avoid pressing hard or holding the iron too long in any one place.

# Cap

*For adult head sizes 20 to 22.*

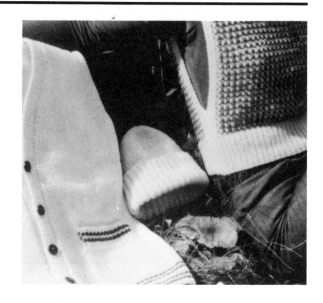

**MATERIALS**

1 4-ounce skein of knitting worsted

1 pair No. 9 straight knitting needles

**Gauge:** 9 stitches = 2 inches.

Starting at bottom, cast on 120 stitches.

**Row 1:** Knit 2, purl 2, repeat from * across row. Repeat this row until piece measures 6 inches. Working in all knit now, work as follows:

**Next Row:** * Knit 1, knit 2 together, repeat from * across row—80 stitches remain.

Now work even, knitting all stitches until piece measures 9 inches in all. Decrease as follows:

**1st Decrease Row:** * Knit 8, knit 2 together, repeat from * across row—72 stitches remain.

**Next Row:** Work even.

**2nd Decrease Row:** * Knit 7, knit 2 together, repeat from * across row—64 stitches remain.

**Next Row:** Work even.

**3rd Decrease Row:** * Knit 6, knit 2 together, repeat from * across row—56 stitches remain.

**Next Row:** Work even.

Continue now in same manner to decrease 8 stitches evenly spaced on each row, having 1 stitch less between each point of decrease, until 8 stitches remain.

Break off yarn, leaving a long thread. Draw yarn tightly through remaining stitches on needle, then sew back seam, sewing on wrong side of row to within 3 inches of bottom, and then on right side along portion of cap which becomes the turnover cuff.

# Slipover

## MATERIALS

4 (5, 6, 6, 7, 7) 4-ounce skeins of knitting worsted
1 pair each of No. 7 and No. 9 straight knitting
    needles

**Pattern Stitch:**

**Row 1:** * Knit 2, purl 2, repeat from * across row.

**Row 2:** Knit.

Repeat these 2 rows for pattern stitch.

**Gauge:** 5 Stitches on No. 9 needles = 1 inch.

**Back:** With No. 9 needles, cast on 84 (88, 92, 96, 100, 106) stitches. Work even in pattern (ending with knit 2 on Row 1 of size 20 only) until piece measures 15 (15, 15½, 15½, 16, 16) inches, or desired length to underarm, ending with a wrong-side row. **Shape Armholes:** Bind off 6 stitches at the beginning of each of the next 2 rows, then, being sure to maintain the pattern as established, work 1 row even, then decrease 1 stitch at the beginning and end of the next row and repeat this decrease every other row 4 (3, 3, 4, 4, 4) times more. Work even now on 62 (68, 72, 74, 78, 84) stitches until piece measures 7 (7¼, 7½, 7¾, 8, 8¼) inches above start of armhole

shaping, ending with a wrong-side row. **Shape Shoulders:** Bind off 10 (11, 12, 12, 13, 14) stitches at the beginning of each of the next 4 rows. Bind off loosely remaining 22 (24, 24, 26, 26, 28) stitches for back of neck.

**Front:** Work in same manner as for back until piece measures 5 (5¼, 5½, 5¾, 6, 6¼) inches above start of armhole shaping, ending with a wrong-side row. **Shape Neck:** Work across 23 (25, 27, 27, 29, 31) stitches, join another ball of yarn, bind off center 16 (18, 18, 20, 20, 22) stitches and work across 23 (25, 27, 27, 29, 31) stitches of other side. Working on both sides at once, decrease 1 stitch at neck edge every other row 3 times. Work even now on 20 (22, 24, 24, 26, 28) stitches of each side until piece measures same as back to shoulders. Shape shoulders as on back.

**Sleeves:** With No. 7 needles, cast on 40 (40, 44, 44, 44, 44) stitches. Knit 1, purl 1 in ribbing for 2½ inches. Change to No. 9 needles and pattern stitch. Work even for 1 inch, then, being sure to maintain the pattern as established, increase 1 stitch at the beginning and end of the next row and repeat this increase every 1 inch 8 (9, 9, 10, 11, 12) times more. Work even now on 58 (60,

64, 66, 68, 70) stitches until piece measures 17½ (18, 18, 18, 18½, 18½) inches, or desired length to underarm. **Shape Cap:** Bind off 6 stitches at the beginning of each of the next 2 rows, then decrease 1 stitch at the beginning and end of every other row for 3 (3¼, 3½, 3¾, 4, 4¼) inches. Bind off 2 stitches at the beginning of each of the next 6 rows. Bind off remaining stitches.

**Finishing:** Sew left shoulder seam. **Neckband:** With No. 7 needles and right side of work facing you, pick up and knit 73 (75, 77, 79, 81, 83) stitches around the neck. Knit 1, purl 1 in ribbing for 1½ inches. Bind off loosely in ribbing. Sew right shoulder seam. Sew short ends of neckband together. Sew side and sleeve seams. Sew in sleeves. Block.

# Vest

*Directions are written for women's size 10. Changes for sizes 12, 14, 16, 18, and 20 are in parentheses.*

## MATERIALS

2 (2, 2, 3, 3, 3) 4-ounce skeins white (Main Color) and 1 (1, 1, 2, 2, 2) taupe (Contrast Color) knitting worsted

1 pair each of No. 7 and No. 9 straight knitting needles

**Pattern Stitch:**

**Row 1:** With MC (Main Color), knit.

**Row 2:** With MC, purl.

**Row 3:** With CC (Contrast Color), knit 1, * slip 1 stitch as if to purl, knit 1, repeat from * across row.

**Row 4:** With CC, * knit 1, slip 1 stitch as if to purl, repeat from * across row.

Repeat these 4 rows for pattern stitch.

**Gauge:** 5 stitches on No. 9 needles = 1 inch.

**Back:** With MC and No. 7 needles, cast on 65 (69, 75, 79, 85, 89) stitches. Knit 1, purl 1 in ribbing for 2¾ inches. Bind off 6 (6, 8, 8, 10, 10) stitches at the beginning of each of the next 2 rows. **Next row (Right Side):** Change to No. 9 needles and pattern stitch. Work even in pattern on 53 (57, 63, 67, 73, 77) stitches until piece measures 17 (17½, 18, 18½, 19, 19½) inches in all, or desired length to shoulder. **Shape Shoulders:** Bind off 8 (9, 10, 11, 12, 13) stitches at the beginning of each of the next 2 rows, then bind off 8 (8, 9, 9, 10, 10) stitches at the beginning of each of the next 2 rows. Bind off loosely remaining 21 (23, 25, 27, 29, 31) stitches for back of neck.

**Front:** Work in ribbing as for back for 2¾ inches. **Next Row** (Right Side): Work in ribbing across 1st 6 (6, 8, 8, 10, 10) stitches and slip these stitches onto a pin to be worked later. Change to No. 9 needles and work in pattern on next 53 (57, 63, 67, 73, 77) stitches, then slip remaining 6 (6, 8, 8, 10, 10) stitches onto another pin to be worked later. Continuing to work now in pattern on the center 53 (57, 63, 67, 73, 77) stitches, work even until piece measures 12 (12½, 13, 13½, 14, 14½) inches **or** 5 inches less than the back measurement from bottom to shoulder, then **Shape Neck:** Work across 19 (20, 22, 23, 25, 26) stitches, join another ball of yarn, bind off center 15 (17, 19, 21, 23, 25) stitches and work across 19 (20, 22, 23, 25, 26) stitches of other side. Working on both sides at once, decrease 1 stitch at each neck edge every other row 3 times. Work even now on 16 (17, 19, 20, 22, 23) stitches of each side until piece measures same as back to shoulders. Shape shoulders as on back.

**Finishing:** Sew left shoulder seam. With MC and No. 7 needles and right side of work facing, pick up and knit 88 (92, 94, 96, 98, 100) stitches around neck. Knit 1, purl 1 in ribbing for 5 rows. Bind off loosely in ribbing. Join other shoulder. Slip 6 (6, 8, 8, 10, 10) stitches from one pin onto No. 7 needles and continue with MC, work in ribbing as established until piece measures up front and down back to point where back ribbing begins. Bind off. Sew in place along side edges, and seam to top of back ribbing. Work 6 (6, 8, 8, 10, 10) stitches of 2nd group of ribbed stitches in same manner. Sew bottom side seams to a point 2 inches above top of bottom ribbing.

# Sleeveless Cardigan

*Directions are written for men's size small (36–38). Changes for medium (40–42) and large (44–46) are in parentheses.*

## MATERIALS

5 (5, 6) 4-ounce skeins white (Main Color) and 1 (1, 1) 2-ounce skein taupe (Contrast Color) knitting worsted

1 pair each of No. 7 and No. 9 straight knitting needles

**Gauge:** 5 stitches on No. 9 needles = 1 inch.

**Back:** With MC and No. 7 needles, cast on 95 (105, 115) stitches. Knit 1, purl 1 in ribbing in color pattern as follows: * 2 rows MC, 2 rows CC, repeat from * once, then work 4 rows MC, and * 2 rows CC, 2 rows MC and repeat from * once. Change to No. 9 needles and stockinette stitch (Knit 1 row, purl 1 row), and work even until piece measures 16 inches in all, ending with a wrong-side row. **Shape Armholes:** Bind off 5 (7, 9) stitches at the beginning of each of the next 2 rows. Work 1 row even, then decrease 1 stitch at the beginning and end of the next row and repeat this decrease every other row 3 (4, 5) times more. Work even now on 77 (81, 85) stitches until piece measures 9½ (10, 10½) inches above start of armhole shaping, ending with a wrong-side row. **Shape Shoulders:** Bind off 12 (13, 14) stitches at the beginning of the next 2 rows, then

bind off 11 (12, 13) stitches at the beginning of the next 2 rows. Bind off loosely remaining 31 stitches for back of neck.

**Right Front:** With MC and No. 7 needles, cast on 58 (63, 68) stitches. Work in color ribbing as on back. **Next Row** (Right Side): Change to No. 9 needles and stockinette stitch. Work across 48 (53, 58) stitches and slip remaining 10 stitches onto a pin to be worked later for front band. Work even on 48 (53, 58) stitches until piece measures 15 inches in all, ending at front edge. **Shape V-Neck:** Decrease 1 stitch at beginning of the next row and repeat this decrease every 6th row 3 (5, 7) times more, then every 4th row 12 (10, 8) times, and *at same time* when piece measures same as back to underarm, ending at side edge, shape the armhole as on back. When 23 (25, 27) stitches remain and piece measures same as back to shoulder, ending at side edge, shape the shoulder as on back.

**Left Front:** Work to correspond to Right Front, reversing all shaping and forming a bottom buttonhole on the center 4-row MC ribbing stripe. **To Make Buttonhole:** Starting at front edge, work in ribbing across 4 stitches, bind off 2 stitches and complete row. On return row cast on 2 stitches over those bound off on previous row.

**Finishing:** Sew shoulder seams. **Right Front Band:** Slip 10 stitches from right front pin onto No. 7 needles and with MC work in knit 1, purl 1 ribbing until piece measures to center back of neck. Bind off. **Left Front Band:** Work in same manner as right front band, working in 4 more buttonholes on this piece, the top one 1 inch below the start of V-neck shaping, and the remaining 3 spaced evenly between. Sew bands in place. With MC and No. 7 needles, and with right side of work facing, pick up and knit 124 (130, 136) stitches around each armhole. Bind off on next row. **Pockets** (make 2): With MC and No. 9 needles, cast on 25 (27, 29) stitches. Work as follows: Knit 1, purl 1 in ribbing across 1st 4 stitches, work in stockinette stitch across next 17 (19, 21) stitches, then work remaining 4 stitches in knit 1, purl 1 ribbing. Work in this manner until piece measures 4 (4½, 5) inches, ending with a wrong-side row. Change to No. 7 needles and work in knit 1, purl 1 ribbing on all stitches in following color pattern: 4 rows MC, 2 rows CC, 2 rows MC, 2 rows CC and 2 rows MC. Bind off loosely in ribbing. Sew pockets in position as shown, placing bottom of pockets to meet top of bottom ribbing. Sew buttons on to correspond to buttonholes. Block.

# 5

# Latchet Hooking

Hooked rugs are lovely, and the ones that are made by hand are all the more beautiful because of the personal creative endeavor of those who have made them. They can be high-pile or low-pile, traditional or contemporary in design, and as large or small or as vari-shaped as your own desire dictates. The richness or elegance of the little latchet-hooked area rug that stands at the foot of the bed and the handsome individuality of the room-size free-form masterpiece that covers the floor of the living room belie the fact that only a few simple tools were needed to work with and that the making of them was a totally delightful and pleasurable experience.

While it is true that all the needlecraft arts are a source of great recreational interest and all share the common denominator of being a means by which you can create highly individual and very personal things of your own, it is also true that each craft has its own attraction for a particular personality. Some prefer a hobby which is totally absorbing and requires a great deal of concentration while others prefer to be busy with their hands while engaged in conversation or preoccupied with an interesting film on television. Some like their work to go fast so that they can finish quickly and go on to something else, while others are more painstaking and want to produce a finer piece of work. It is for these reasons that many are busy with so many types of crafts, one of the most popular ones among them being the type of work that can be done with a latchet hook, some yarn, and a piece of canvas.

To work with the latchet hook is easy, and it is one of the crafts in which little concentration is required. Your stitches are outlined and al-

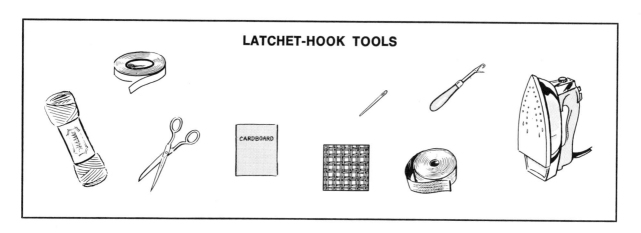

ready gauged for you on the large openings of the woven canvas which serves as the background for latchet-hook work, and because of this there cannot be any reason for uneven tension or other irregularity in your work. It is also because of the completely controlled tension in this craft that the work can be picked up by anyone at any time and carried on—a change of hand in the work will never show.

Latchet hooking is one of the hobbies which a friend or another member of the family can work on together with you, and a partially worked canvas spread on a bridge table is an invitation for one or two to sit down and while talking or listening to music quietly work the latch hook down under, up again, and then back again through the spaces on the canvas—as compulsive an experience almost as that of picking potato chips out of a snack bowl, yet certainly a much more creative and productive one.

We have spoken so far only of latchet-hooked rugs, but many other original things can also be made, such as throw pillows, tote bags, wall hangings, and furry little clothing accessories. The method of working any latchet-hook project is always the same, and you may use any charted design or devise an interesting one of your own. Along with each of our designs, we offer suggestions for other things that can be made and how to make rugs to smaller or larger sizes if you so desire. By carefully observing the details outlined in the General Instructions, you should be able to have beautiful results with whatever latchet-hook project you attempt.

## LATCHET-HOOK STITCH

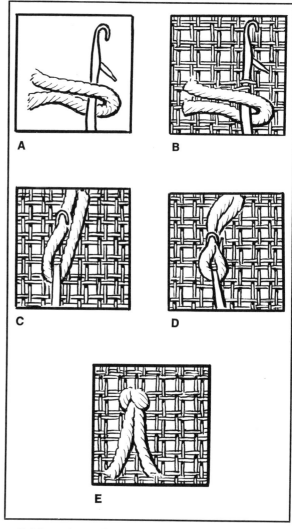

Fold a piece of yarn in half over the shank of your hook, just below the latch, **A.** Holding the two ends of yarn evenly between the thumb and index finger of your left hand, and using your right index finger to hold the latch down, insert the hook under two horizontal threads of your canvas and up through the space directly above, having the latch now above the horizontal threads. Draw the hook lightly toward you until the latch is at a right angle to the shank, **B.** Bring yarn ends over the shank of the hook now between the latch and the hooked end, **C,** and pull hook through canvas, drawing ends of yarn through loop, **D.** Pull loose ends to tighten, **E.**

## GENERAL INSTRUCTIONS

Rug canvas is a large open-mesh material, usually consisting of 4 open spaces to 1 inch. In this type of work, each space or box represents 1 stitch. Each color to be filled into each box is indicated in the patterns by a symbol shown at the top of the patterns and repeated on the individual charts accompanying each design. The selvedge edge (or edges) on a piece of canvas indicates a side edge, rather than a top or bottom edge.

Many kinds of yarn can be used for your latchet-hook work and the only real prerequisites are that you buy yarn of good enough quality to endure enough wear and tear to merit the amount of creative effort you are putting into your work, and that it is of a heavy enough gauge to cover evenly the open-mesh spaces of your background canvas. Cotton, wool, or synthetic rug yarns are good to use, as are bulky yarns of any type, and also yarns of knitting worsted weight. For our designs we have used a good quality of knitting worsted weight wool and have used double strands of yarn for each stitch to achieve extra pile and thickness for our rugs.

The length of the strands of yarn you use determines the height of the pile in your finished product. Many yarns for latchet-hook work come in precut bundles in which each strand is usually cut to 2½ inches in length, and these give a good texture to your work and are fine to use. If, however, you feel that you prefer to use a yarn other than that which you can buy precut, then your easy alternative is to buy whatever yarn you choose in wound skeins, and either use one of the automatic rug yarn cutters available in most yarn stores, or cut a small cardboard model for the actual size you want, wind your yarn several times around it, and then cut and make up your own precut bundles. We have used 3-inch strands of yarn for our models.

If you prefer to cut your own yarn, separate your small strands by color as they are cut, putting them into individual packets or small open boxes. This will make your work easier since, needing to work strand by strand, you will find that your colors have not become mixed to the point where you have to stop to separate them as you work.

In working your stitches, it is best to work from one side margin to the other, and from the bottom up, always keeping the finished portion of the work nearest to you so that, in working more of the pattern, your hook does not catch into stitches already completed. If two people are working on the rug at the same time, it is preferable for each to start at a different side edge and work toward the center.

The amount of rug canvas needed for our designs is also indicated in the directions. This amount allows for 6 free boxes on each of the 4 sides, 4 of them (approximately 1 inch) to be used for hemming, and the balance cut away.

There are two methods of hemming. One is to turn the free boxes to what will be the wrong side of your work before you start, miter the corners, then firmly press the edges, and when you do your rug, work the 4 end stitches on each of the 4 sides through the double thickness of the right side of the canvas and the turned-under hem. The second way, which we prefer, is to seal the 4 edges of your cut canvas with masking tape to prevent their raveling, then work your design within the margin of the free borders, and when your rug is completed, miter the corners, turn your borders to the wrong side of the work, and then hem them into place.

When your rug is done, shake it well to clear it of any yarn-end dust and trim it to an even pile by clipping any long ends. Final finishing is done with rug binding 1 to 1½ inches wide, placed on the wrong side of the work over the turned-under hem portion. Rug binding is available in both the sew-on and the iron-on varieties. Either type is good, and complete directions accompany the package containing whichever type you buy.

*Note:* We have used wool of knitting worsted weight for our rugs, and have used 2 3-inch strands for each stitch and canvas with 4 spaces to 1 inch. For color and design follow the directions shown on whichever chart describes the rug you want to make.

# Gingham Plaid Rug

*Approximate finished size 24 x 34 inches.*

## MATERIALS

3 4-ounce skeins each of white and deep purple
    and 5 4-ounce skeins of lilac
      knitting worsted
Rug canvas 27 inches wide x 37 inches long
Latchet hook

**Finish** rug in manner described under General Instructions.

This rug can be easily enlarged by working a deep purple border of desired width around the entire outer edge, or by widening the deep purple

stripes that run throughout the pattern. It can be made smaller by eliminating half or all of each of the tweed and lilac squares which form the outer edges of the rug as now designed. Any portion of the pattern may be used for making a *tote bag* or a *pillow*. In changing the original design in any of the suggested ways, it is most important to remember to count the number of boxes that you will be using on your own design, and to remember that every 4 boxes equals 1 inch. This will help you to determine how large your new piece will be and will tell you how much canvas you will need to work with.

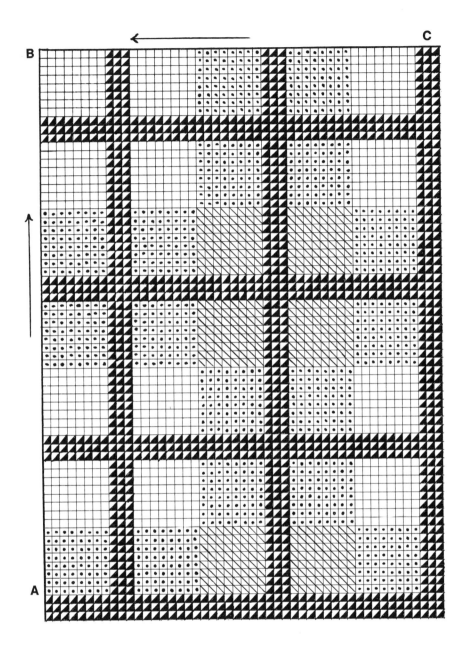

COLOR KEY

TWEED
DEEP PURPLE
WHITE
LILAC

# Vari-Striped Rug

*Approximate finished size 28 x 38 inches.*

## MATERIALS

3 4-ounce skeins each of white, lilac and light
   green and 10 4-ounce skeins of deep purple
   knitting worsted
Rug canvas 31 inches wide x 41 inches long
Latchet hook

**Finish** rug in manner described under General
Instructions.

A variation on this rug would be to make it
wider by adding 1, 2, or 3 more stitches to the
width of each stripe, or to all the stripes of one
or two colors only. The rug can be made longer
by lengthening each of the stripes between each
of the wider deep purple stripes. Should you
want the rug smaller, change the pattern by
eliminating some of the stripes altogether, and
shortening the length of each of the stripes between the deep purple ones. A stunning *cinch
belt* or *clutch bag* could be made from any portion of this striped pattern. Again, in changing to
any design other than ours, you would need only
to follow the few simple rules outlined at the
bottom of the directions for the gingham plaid
rug.

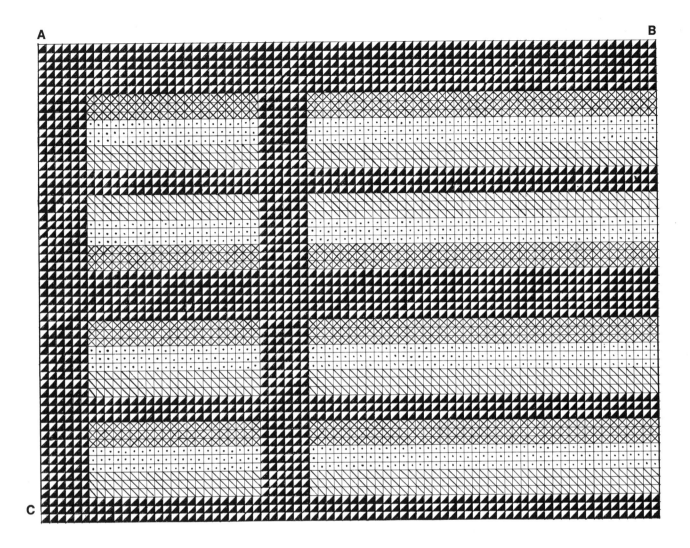

**COLOR KEY**

◤ DEEP PURPLE

⊠ LIGHT GREEN

⊡ LILAC

◺ WHITE

# Pinwheel Rug

*Approximate finished size 24 inches in diameter.*

## MATERIALS

3 4-ounce skeins each of white, lilac and deep
purple knitting worsted
Rug canvas 30 inches square
Latchet hook

This rug, being a round one, is worked in just
a little different way than described under the
General Instructions. Tape the edges of the 4
sides of your square canvas, rather than attempt
to work through a double thickness around the
outer edge of the circle. The rug should be
worked, one color at a time, from the outer edge
toward the center, and the way to start it is to
have the center stitch of the widest part of whichever of the 9 segments you choose to work first
placed 6 spaces in from the outer edge of the

square canvas in the center of any of the 4 sides.
When your work is completed, **finish** it in the
following way: Cut away any excess canvas remaining on each of the 4 corners, leaving a
border now of 6 free spaces around the whole
outer edge of your completed work. Turn this
edge to the wrong side of the rug and tack into
place, cutting into the canvas where necessary to
make it conform to shape. Press or sew on rug
binding, cutting into it as necessary to achieve
the round shape. Overlap the cut edges and either
sew or iron them into place so that the final underside finish is neat.

Because of the special intricacy of the design
of this particular pattern, it is suggested that you
do not attempt to deviate from the pattern as
it is given.

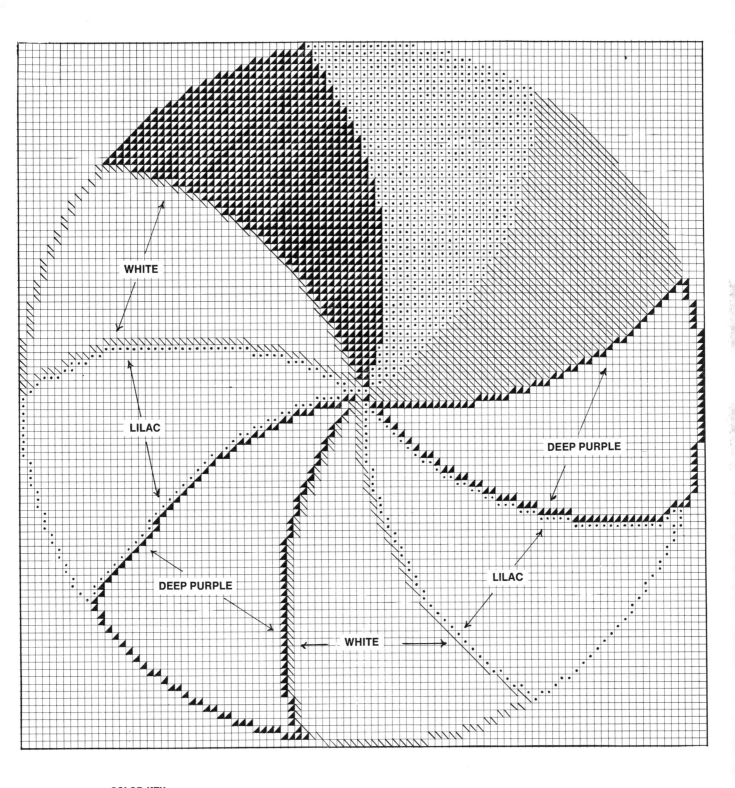

WHITE

LILAC

DEEP PURPLE

DEEP PURPLE

WHITE

LILAC

**COLOR KEY**
DEEP PURPLE
LILAC
WHITE

# 6

# Macramé

Fishermen who in ancient times were ingenious enough to discover that the weaving and knotting of natural fibers was a means of making sturdy nets with which to haul in their catch from the sea could not possibly have envisioned how their very basic techniques would be used as a popular art form in the twentieth century. Only comparatively recently have people become aware of the very interesting decorative accessories that can be designed by making a series of simple knots in twine, cord, or any similar material that is available. The fishermen's craft has interested others before now, but in a different sort of way. Among the staunchest early enthusiasts were seamen who found the making of different kinds of knots a fascinating way of filling long empty hours while at sea, and who found good use for their knotted ropes in making lanyards with which to hold spars and cargo in place.

Arabian weavers in the 13th century had discovered that instead of cutting off leftover lengths of cords or strings on the edges of their woven goods, they could knot or braid these leftover lengths into decorative fringes. Their name for this type of ornamental trimming was *migramah,* the source of the word macramé.

The art as we know it today is a very fascinating hobby that is worked with just a few materials, which are inexpensive and easy to find, and that can be perfected by practicing the making of a few knots which can be tied in infinite pattern arrangements to make a stunning variety of objects. Little or practically no instruction is necessary to become accomplished in this art. Once you have learned how to make just one or two kinds of knots, you can develop your

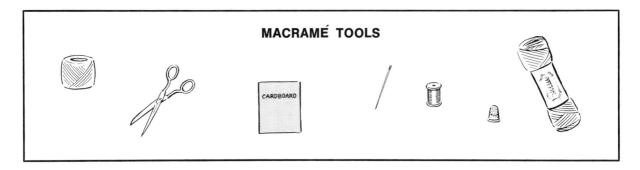

## MACRAMÉ TOOLS

own ideas as to the various cord, color, and design combinations needed to create all sorts of unusual things.

This simple craft that helped seamen to while away their idle hours serves in the same way to fill the many leisure hours that people have today. Time passes quickly as one becomes absorbed with the knotting process. So relaxing is this absorption that it has been found to be a great aid to those who are confined in hospitals and other institutions and who have much free time to fill and a desire to do something constructive with that time.

Once you have tried your hand at macramé, you will realize how very rewarding your endeavors in this particular craft can be. We hope that you will find pleasure in working out some of the patterns offered, and that you will be sufficiently inspired, after you have made them, to go on designing new things of your own.

## MACRAMÉ STITCHES OR KNOTS

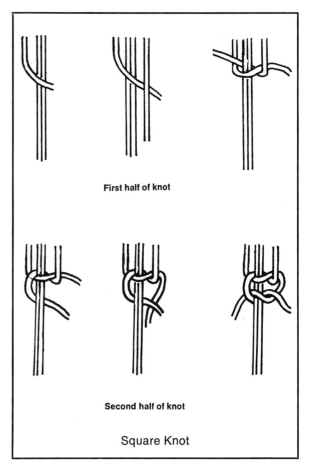

**First half of knot**

**Second half of knot**

Square Knot

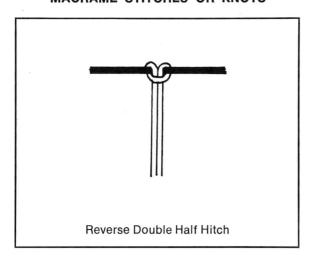

Reverse Double Half Hitch

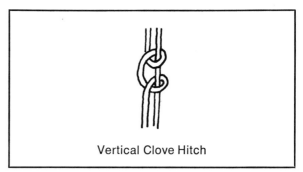

Vertical Clove Hitch

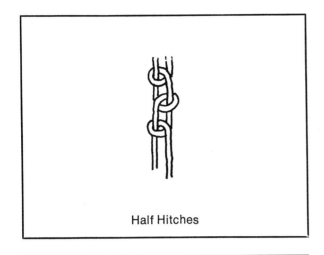

Half Hitches

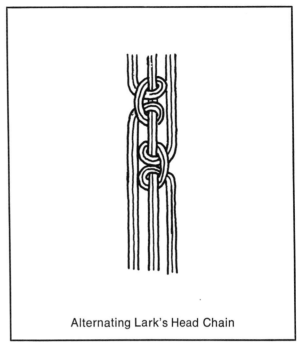

Alternating Lark's Head Chain

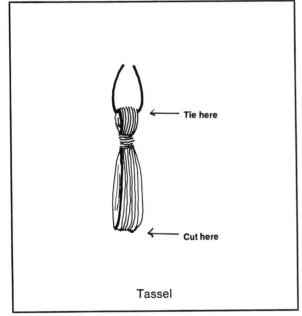

Tie here

Cut here

Tassel

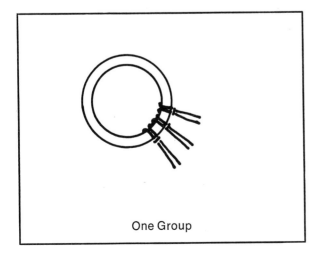

One Group

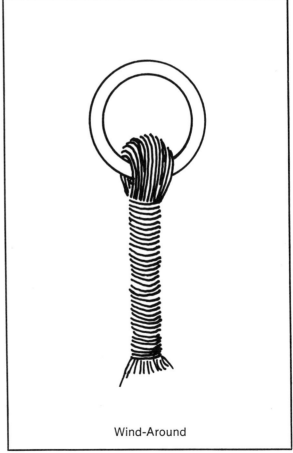

Wind-Around

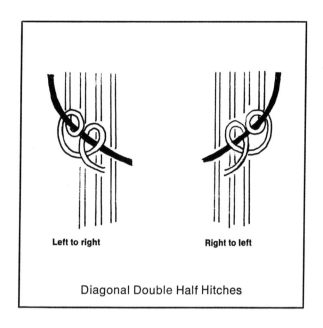

**Left to right**      **Right to left**

Diagonal Double Half Hitches

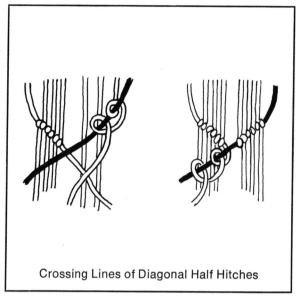

Crossing Lines of Diagonal Half Hitches

## GENERAL INSTRUCTIONS

Assemble your materials before you begin your macramé work, and test the materials you have bought to be sure that they are colorfast and shrinkproof.

Your working surface may be a foam rubber pad, a square of Celotex or soft pine wood, or just a piece of thick cardboard held to a clipboard. Attach your work with pins, thumbtacks, or tape.

Roll your cut yarns onto bobbins or into balls secured with rubber bands. This will make it easier for you to work.

In the directions for our designs, we specify yarn amounts. If you should design a project of your own, remember that the cording lengths you use should be eight times longer than the item

you are planning to make. For example, if you want to make something that is 1 yard long, each cording must measure 8 yards. It is always safer to have some cording left over rather than to run short before your item is finished; it is virtually impossible to add new lengths without having the joinings show.

It is wise to practice the knots you plan to use on a small piece before starting on any major project. This will familiarize you with the particular knotting process and help you to be sufficiently relaxed to maintain a smooth and even tension in your work.

When one or more *asterisks* (*) appear in the directions, repeat whatever follows the asterisk or asterisks as many times as specified. When *parentheses* ( ) occur, repeat whatever is written within the parentheses as many times as specified.

# Placemat

## MATERIALS

100 yards of skipper blue (Main Color) and 70 yards of light aqua (Contrast Color) heavy acrylic rug yarn

Cut 16 strands MC (Main Color) and 12 strands CC (Contrast Color), each to measure 5 yards. Cut 1 strand of either color to measure 18 inches for the foundation cord and attach this to the working surface. Fold strands in half and attach with reverse double half hitches to the foundation cord as follows (4 MC and 4 CC) 3 times, then 4 MC once more.

Leaving 3 inches free below the foundation line, start knotting as follows:

**Row 1:** * Make a square knot over the next 4 strands. Repeat from * across.

**Row 2:** Skip the 1st 2 strands, then make a * square knot over the next 4 strands. Repeat from * across, skip the last 2 strands.

** Stripe (Rows 3, 4, and 5):

**Row 3:** Using the 1st strand as the knot-bearing strand and working from left to right, make diagonal half hitches with 2nd, 3rd, and 4th strands. Using the 8th strand as the knot-bearing strand and working from right to left, make diagonal half hitches with the 7th, 6th, and 5th strands.

**Row 4:** Leaving ¾ inch free below last diagonal half hitches, make a square knot using the 1st and 8th strands to tie around the center 6 strands.

**Row 5:** Leaving ¾ inch free below the square knot and using the 4th strand as the knot-bearing strand, make diagonal half hitches from right to left with the 3rd, 2nd, and 1st strands. Using the 5th strand as the knot-bearing strand and working from left to right, make diagonal half hitches from left to right with the 6th, 7th, and 8th strands. Repeat stripe section from ** across.

**Row 6:** *** Skip 7 strands, make a square knot with the next 2 strands (these are the knot-bearing strands). Repeat from *** across.

**Row 7:** **** Using the 1st strand as the knot-bearing strand and working from left to right, make diagonal half hitches with the 2nd, 3rd, and 4th strands. Using the 8th strand as the knot-bearing strand and working from right to left, make diagonal half hitches with the 7th, 6th, and 5th strands. Repeat from **** across.

Repeat Row 4 to Row 7 twice more.

Now repeat Rows 4 and 5.

**Next Row:** Repeat Row 2.

**Last Row:** Repeat Row 1.

Leaving 3-inch fringe, cut off remainder of the strands. Trim fringe at other end to correspond.

# Macramé Pillow

## MATERIALS

65 yards of medium green (Main Color) and 35 yards of light turquoise (Contrast Color) rayon and cotton rug yarn

12-inch square pillow form

½ yard of lining material in Contrast Color

Cut 32 strands MC (Main Color), each to measure 66 inches. Cut one more piece to measure 24 inches for foundation cord and attach this piece to the working surface. Fold the 66-inch lengths in half and attach to the foundation cord with reverse double half hitches. The row should measure 24 inches. Leaving 2 inches free below the foundation line, start knotting as follows:

**Row 1:** * Make a square knot over the next 4 strands. Repeat from * across. Leave ½ inch free below this row of knots.

**Row 2:** Skip the first 2 strands, * make a square knot over the next 4 strands. Repeat from * across and skip the last 2 strands. Leave ½ inch free below this row of knots.

**Rows 3, 4, and 5:** Repeat Row 1. Leave ¾ inch free below this row of knots.

**Row 6:** Repeat Row 1. Leave ½ inch free below this row of knots.

**Rows 7 and 8:** Make one half hitch over the first 2 strands, * make a square knot over the next 4 strands and repeat from * across. Make one half hitch over the last 2 strands. Leave ½ inch free below this row of knots.

**Rows 9, 10, and 11:** Repeat Row 1. Leave ¾ inch free below this row of knots.

**Row 12:** Repeat Row 1. Leave ½ inch free below this row of knots.

**Row 13:** Repeat Row 2. Leave ½ inch free below this row of knots.

**Row 14:** Repeat Row 1. Trim ends to measure 2 inches.

**Finishing:** Cut 2 pieces of fabric, each to measure 14 inches square. Seam 2 side edges of fabric and place on the pillow form, leaving the top and bottom open. Stretch knotted piece over the covered pillow form, seaming it at center back and leaving the loose ends extending beyond the pillow at top and bottom. Sew top and bottom seams, tucking in the extended loose ends of knotted piece as you sew. **Tassels** (make 4): Wind CC (Contrast Color) yarn 20 times around a 7-inch piece of cardboard. Draw one 12-inch length under the strands at one end and tie securely. Slip yarn from cardboard and cut strands at opposite end. Wind another 12-inch length 4 times around the tassel, 1¼ inches below the tied end and fasten securely. Trim evenly. Sew one tassel to each corner of the pillow.

# Plant Hanger

## MATERIALS

1 ball smooth hard-finish twine
2 plastic rings 2 inches in diameter

Cut 10 strands each to measure 4¾ yards and 5 strands each to measure 2¾ yards. Fold strands in half and attach with reverse double half hitches to one plastic ring as follows: * 1 long strand, 1 short strand, 1 long strand (*see* One Group stitch illustration). This forms a group of 6 working strands. Repeat from * 4 times more to make 5 groups in all.

**First Group:** Work lark's head chain, alternating the 2 strands at left over the center 2 strands, then the 2 strands at right over the center 2 strands. Continue in this manner until piece measures 17 inches from plastic ring. Work remaining 4 groups in the same manner. Trim ends to measure 7 inches from the last knots. Draw ends through other plastic ring, overlapping 3 inches. Wind a single strand of twine tightly around cords reaching from plastic ring down to last knots (*see* Wind-Around stitch illustration). Fasten securely.

# Wall Hanging

## MATERIALS

200 yards rayon and cotton rug yarn
½-inch diameter dowel rod, 24 inches long
21 beads with ¼-inch beading hole
Metal chain of desired length for hanging

Cut 50 strands each to measure 4 yards. Fold strands in half and attach with reverse double half hitch to the dowel rod, leaving ½ inch free at each end of rod. *Do not wind yarn into balls for this design. Leave strands hanging free.* Start knotting from left as follows:

**First Quarter of Diamond:** Skip 1st strand. Using the 9th strand as the knot-bearing strand, work the diagonal double half hitch from right to left. Leave the 8th strand hanging at back of work. Make diagonal double half hitch with the 7th, 6th, 5th, 4th, 3rd, and 2nd strands.

**Second Quarter of Diamond:** Using the 8th strand as the knot-bearing strand, work the diagonal double half hitch from left to right. Make diagonal double half hitches with the 10th, 11th,

12th, 13th, 14th, and 15th strands. * Skip 6 strands and leave the 7th strand hanging at back of the work (to be used later as a knot-bearing strand). Using the 8th strand as the knot-bearing strand and working from right to left, make diagonal double half hitches with the 6th, 5th, 4th, 3rd, 2nd, and 1st strands. Using the 7th strand as the knot bearing strand now and working from left to right, make diagonal double half hitches with the 9th, 10th, 11th, 12th, 13th, and 14th strands. Repeat from * across. There are 7 diamonds on the row. Skip the last strand. Knot the free strand at each edge to the adjacent knot-bearing strand with a vertical clove hitch. Thread the center 6 strands of each diamond through a bead.

**Third Quarter of Diamond:** Skip the 1st 2 strands. ** Use the next strand as the knot-bearing strand, and work the diagonal double half hitch from left to right. Make diagonal double half hitches with the next 2 strands, then with the first 3 strands of the center 6 strands emerging from the bead.

**Fourth Quarter of Diamond:** Skip the knot-bearing strand at the right side of diamond. Use the next strand to the left of the skipped strand as the new knot-bearing strand and work the diagonal double half hitch from right to left. Make diagonal double half hitches with the next 2 strands, then with the remaining 3 strands emerging from the bead. Cross the knot-bearing strands at the bottom of the diamond (*see* Crossing Lines of Diagonal Half Hitches illustration). Skip the next 2 knot-bearing strands. Repeat from ** across, skipping the last 2 strands at the right edge.

**Fill In Diamonds:** Skip the first strand at the left edge. Make a square knot over the next 4 strands, placing the knot on a level with the crossed strands. Skip the next 2 strands. Where diamonds touch each other * make a vertical clove hitch with the old knot-bearing strand of the **Second Quarter** of the first diamond and the old knot-bearing strand of the **First Quarter** of the second diamond. *** Skip the next 8 strands, make a square knot over the next 4 strands, placing the knot ½ inch below the vertical clove hitch; make a square knot with the last 2 skipped strands and the following 2 strands of the square knot just made, ½ inch below the previous knot; make a square knot with the next 4 strands to the right, in line with the previous knot; then another square knot with the center 4 strands ½ inch below the previous knots. Repeat from *** across, ending with a square knot with the 4 strands next to the last strand. Repeat from **First Quarter of Diamond** once more, then make 1 more row of diamonds.

**Fringe:** Leaving 3 inches free below the last row of vertical clove hitches, make a square knot over the first 8 strands, then make another square knot immediately below this knot (make 2 square knots in this manner out of the next 14 strands) 6 times; make 2 square knots over the last 8 strands. Trim fringe evenly 6 inches below the last square knots. Attach hanging chain to either side of dowel rod.

# Needlepoint and Bargello

Needlepoint is a beautiful picture art that has been enjoyed through the centuries. Easy to do, it requires just a little skill and only a few working materials. Patience is the only real demand upon those who choose to do this kind of work, and although patience is always a virtue, in this particular instance it does indeed carry its own reward. The end result of one's stitch-by-stitch drawing with a needle and yarn onto a piece of canvas mesh is a work of art to be proud of and a creation to be handed down to following generations as a family treasure.

Some people prefer to buy preworked pieces of canvas in which the intricate focal design has already been done, and they find their pleasure in filling in the background portion and watching the design grow into its true setting as they work. Others like to work with a printed canvas on which the complete pattern and its colors are marked out for them to follow. Still others want to draw their own design on plain canvas, choose their colors, and then follow their own ideas for a completely original piece. Whichever of these ways one wants to work, the pleasure can be great, the end result gratifying, and the kinds of things one can make is just as varied, ranging from pillows, wall hangings, chair seat covers, and all types of home accessories to slippers, purses, belts, and other more personal things.

Needlepoint is a generic term which includes, in addition to the "needlepoint" we speak of which is worked on a canvas having anywhere between 10 and 18 meshes to an inch, such techniques as *petit point* which is very fine and worked on a canvas having at least 20 meshes to an inch; *gros point,* generally done on canvas

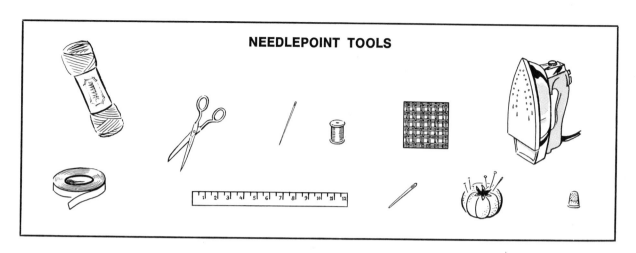

## NEEDLEPOINT TOOLS

having between 8 and 12 meshes to an inch, and *quick point,* on canvas between 3 and 7 meshes to an inch. The method of working in these various types of needlepoint is always the same, but petit point is rather delicate work done with fine thread on fine canvas and requires more dexterity and patience than either gros point or quick point, which are worked with heavy yarn and more open canvas and go much quicker. Many of the designs worked in either gros point or quick point are bright and bold and quite stunning, but the designs cannot be as intricate and detailed as in the finer work since obviously there are not enough spaces or stitches available.

Bargello is another form of the "needlepoint" you will be doing, worked with the same needle and the same type of yarn and canvas. The difference between this very popular age-old craft, originally used by upholsterers for covering furniture, and needlepoint is that a needlepoint stitch is worked into each and every space on the background canvas, whereas bargello stitches are worked over two or more spaces at a time and the stitches are always upright and vary with each pattern as to the number of spaces they cover. Those who enjoy doing bargello work like it because it goes quickly and can be done in some very eye-catching designs—quite bold, very colorful, and generally geometric in pattern. The use of needlepoint and bargello in a single piece can be a very wonderful combination, the space-by-space needlepoint stitches working out the form and shape of the design and the bargello stitches

forming an unusual background.

You will enjoy whichever way you choose to work in this craft. Besides its other virtues, needlepoint is a "sociable" art in that it requires little concentration and you can be free to enjoy the company of others while you are engaged in the creation of your masterpiece. It is a "portable" art, too, inasmuch as most needlepoint pieces are small enough to be taken along wherever you go. We hope that you will find the pieces we have designed for you attractive and that, having tried one, you will want to try some others and then perhaps go on to designs of your own.

*Note:* Be certain that your needlepoint materials are of good enough quality to merit the amount of effort you will be putting into your work. Your canvas should have evenly spaced meshes, and the threads should have no irregularities (knots or bumps). The polished, semi-stiff type of canvas is easier to work with and adds body to your finished piece. Your yarn should be colorfast, mothproofed, and of a quality that will not fray or pill as you work it through the canvas mesh. Your needle should be blunt-edged so that it does not catch into stitches that have already been worked, and it should have a slender eye large enough to accommodate the thickness of the yarn you will be using and yet be able to slide smoothly through the meshes of your canvas without separating or distorting them. Any reputable art needlework dealer will be glad to help you select these materials.

# NEEDLEPOINT STITCHES

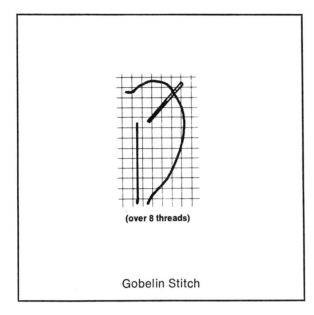

(over 8 threads)

Gobelin Stitch

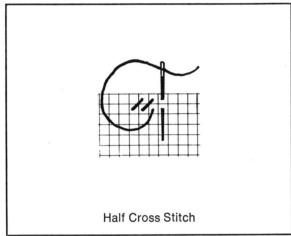

Half Cross Stitch

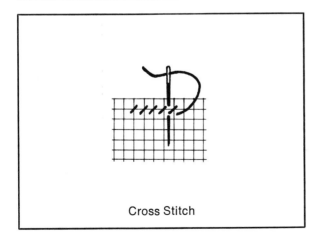

Cross Stitch

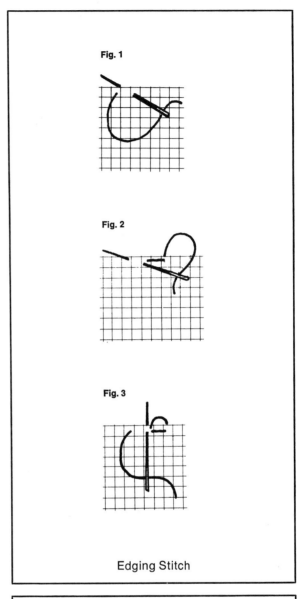

Fig. 1

Fig. 2

Fig. 3

Edging Stitch

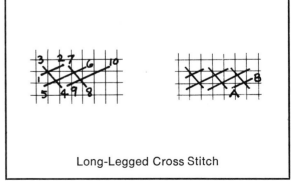

Long-Legged Cross Stitch

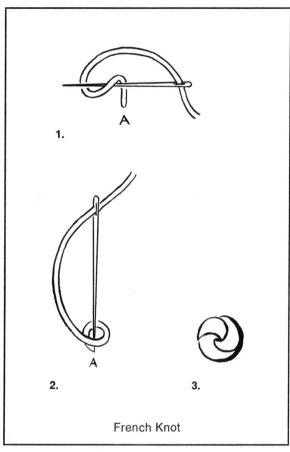

**1.**

**A**

**2.** **A**     **3.**

French Knot

Bring yarn through at dot on **A,** wrap yarn around needle once (as shown) or as many times as desired (1), then pass needle down through fabric at point **A** (2). Completed stitch looks as shown (3).

## GENERAL INSTRUCTIONS

Assemble all your working materials before starting your project. Arrange always to work in good light and manage to be relaxed while you are working. Do not attempt to rush through your project; needlepoint is a relaxed, unhurried art. The tension of your stitches will be smooth and even if you work at a sure and easy pace.

The designs offered are worked on canvas having 10 meshes to an inch. Each background square on the charts accompanying the designs represents one thread of the canvas, with the exception of the sampler on which each line of the chart represents one thread of canvas.

Read your directions carefully, concentrating on one portion of them at a time. It will be confusing and of no value to read any directions before you are actually ready to work them.

Before beginning to stitch, bind the raw edges of the canvas with masking tape to prevent their raveling as you work. If the canvas has selvedge edges, these should be used as side edges.

Cut your yarn to a comfortable working length, usually about 18 inches. A little experimenting will tell you what length is most comfortable for you. Do not let the short end of your yarn extend more than 2 or 3 inches beyond the needle eye. The constant drawing of double yarn through your canvas will cause an uneven tension in your work.

If the yarn twists after you have worked with it for a little while, drop the threaded end and allow the yarn to unwind itself.

Starting your piece of needlepoint, leave a 2-inch or 3-inch strand of yarn free on the wrong side of the work. Work the first 4 or 5 stitches over the free strand in the back, then cut off the remainder of that strand. When coming to the end of a piece of yarn you are working with, draw your needle through to the underside of the work, turn the canvas over and, working on the wrong side, weave your needle over and under every other stitch just completed for about 1 inch, then cut off the remaining end of yarn. To start a new strand, start opposite the previous ending and weave your needle with the new strand over and under every other stitch for about 1 inch.

It is usually necessary to ease a finished piece of needlepoint back into shape by **blocking** it, since the canvas tends to become a little distorted as it is worked. To do your blocking, pin the piece right side up onto a board, being sure to use rustproof pins and to have the corners absolutely at right angles and the parallel sides stretched to exactly the same length. Dampen the canvas and leave it pinned until it is completely dry, then press it lightly, if desired. If you have worked a design of your own that is larger than the pieces described here, secure it to the board with aluminum nails; they hold better than pins.

# Key Ring Tab

**MATERIALS**

2 yards of gold, 3 yards of black, and 6 yards of
    flame knitting worsted

1 4 x 6-inch piece of canvas

No. 18 tapestry needle

Key ring (with chain)

The chart for the Key Ring Tab shows ½ of
the entire piece. For your working area, measure
1 inch down from one short edge and 1 inch in
from the adjacent long edge of the canvas, and
mark with a pin. This is **A** on the Key Ring Tab
Chart. The piece is worked in half cross stitch
and each stitch is worked over 1 thread of canvas.
Work each row from left to right and turn the
canvas upside down at the end of each row.

Following Color Key and, starting at pin on
your canvas, follow the chart to the bottom. Skip
the next 2 horizontal canvas threads, then repeat the chart once more.

**Finishing:** Trim your canvas, leaving 5 threads
free on each of the 4 sides. Place masking tape on
wrong side of each corner. Leaving 1 canvas
thread free for the edge around the 4 sides of
the embroidered piece, fold the raw edges to the
wrong side, miter the corners and then baste
them in place. With double strands of black
yarn, work edging stitch along this edge, and
starting with Figs. 1, 2, and 3, and then repeating
Figs. 2 and 3 alternately. Remove the basting
thread. Fold the canvas at the 2 free canvas
threads, being careful to have the 1st canvas
thread behind the other. With double strands of
black worsted, work edging stitch along this edge,
being careful to use the 2 canvas threads as one.
Insert the end of the chain at any corner and
fasten into place. Sew the remaining 3 sides together.

A ⇨

**COLOR KEY**

| ⊠ | BLACK | ⎫ |
| ☐ | GOLD | ⎬ HALF CROSS STITCH |
| ⊡ | FLAME | ⎭ |

# Tote Bag

## MATERIALS

40 yards each of red and orange and 105 yards of
    black heavy acrylic rug yarn
2 pieces of canvas: 1 piece 21 x 16 inches for the
    bag and 1 piece 6 x 22 inches for the handle
No. 18 tapestry needle
2 pieces of lining material: 1 piece of red 11 x 30
    inches for the bag and 1 piece of black 3 x 22
    inches for the handle
1 piece of black felt, 11 x 6 inches
2 pieces of cardboard

Only half of the canvas will be worked on;
the remainder is used for stiffening. For your
working area, measure 1 inch in from one short
edge, and 10½ inches in from the adjacent long
edge of your canvas, and mark with a pin. This
is **A** on the Tote Bag Chart. The bag is worked
in gobelin stitch, and the handle in half cross
stitch. Work each gobelin stitch over 8 threads
of the canvas, as shown, working each row from
left to right and each half cross stitch over 2
threads of the canvas.

Following Color Key and, starting at pin on
your canvas, work the first row, following chart
from **A** to **B** 15 times. Work the remaining rows

in the same way, following the chart to the bottom. For **monogram** on the handle of the bag,
copy the 3 letters of your monogram from the Alphabet Chart into the 3 blank boxes of the chart
for the handle. Work your monogram in orange
and the remainder of the handle in black. Starting at left on narrow edge, 1 inch in from the
narrow edge and 1 inch in from the adjacent long
edge, follow the chart for the handle until the
monogram has been completed, then repeat the
next row to within 1 inch from the opposite end.

**Finishing:** Turn the embroidered canvas of the
handle to the wrong side, 1 stitch in from each
long edge, and fold the unworked portion of the
canvas to the back for double strength. Line the
handle. Turn the embroidered canvas of the bag
to the wrong side at fold lines as indicated on
the chart. With the unworked portion of the
canvas on the wrong side, sew the side seams. Cut
an oval piece of cardboard, the same shape as the
bottom of the bag. Cut a piece of black felt for
the bottom of the bag and sew it in place on the
canvas. Place the cardboard oval inside the bag
for stiffening the bottom portion. Line the bag
with the red material, inserting one end of the
handle at each oval end of the bag.

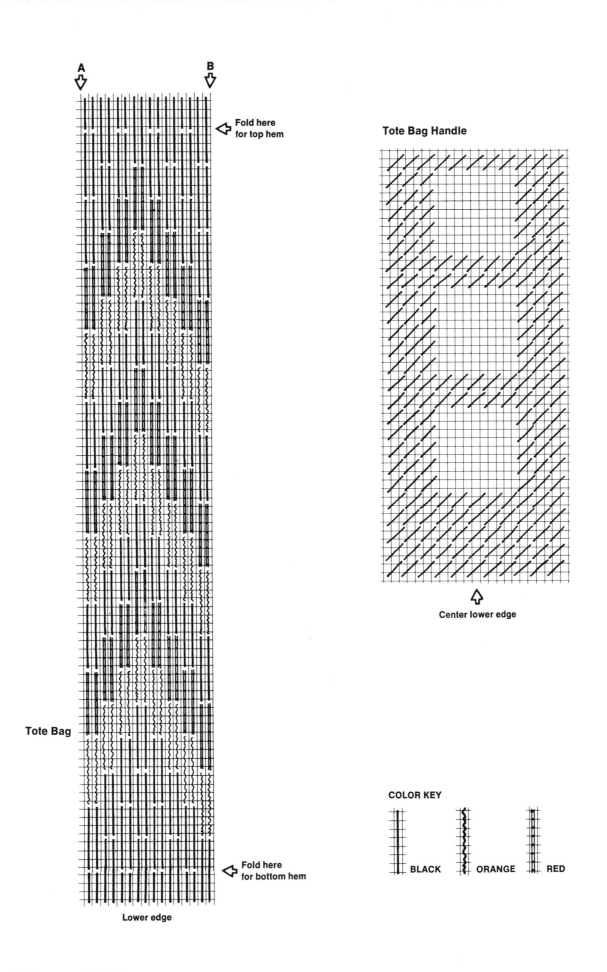

A    B

Fold here
for top hem

**Tote Bag Handle**

Tote Bag

Fold here
for bottom hem

Lower edge

Center lower edge

**COLOR KEY**

BLACK        ORANGE        RED

# Cosmetic Case

**Alphabet Chart**

## MATERIALS

9 yards of flame, 15 yards of gold, and 20 yards of black knitting worsted

1 8½ x 14½-inch piece of canvas

No. 18 tapestry needle

1 7 x 13-inch piece of lining material

The chart for the cosmetic case shows ⅓ of the entire piece. For your working area, measure 1 inch down from one short edge and 1 inch in from the adjacent long edge of canvas, and mark with a pin. This is **A** on the Cosmetic Case Chart. The piece is worked in half cross stitch and each stitch is worked over 1 thread of the canvas. Work each row from left to right and turn the canvas upside down at the end of each row.

Following Color Key and starting at pin on your canvas, follow the chart to the bottom. Skip the next 2 horizontal canvas threads, then repeat the chart once more. Copy the 3 letters of your **monogram** from the Alphabet Chart into the Center Monogram Panel (this is the center rectangular square on the Cosmetic Case Chart). Skip the next 2 horizontal canvas threads and work the chart once more, working your mono-

gram in cross stitch with flame and the background of the monogram in half cross stitch with gold.

**Finishing:** Trim your canvas, leaving 5 threads free on each of the 4 sides. Place masking tape on the wrong side of each corner. Leaving 1 canvas thread free for edging around the 4 sides of the embroidered piece, fold the raw edges of your work to the wrong side, miter the corners (see page 103), and then baste them in place. With double strands of black knitting worsted, work the edging stitch around the outer edges, starting with Figs. 1, 2, and 3 of chart, then repeating Figs. 2 and 3 alternately. Remove the basting thread. Leaving a ¼-inch margin all around, line the embroidered piece. With monogram facing you, fold the canvas along the next 2 free canvas threads, being careful to have the 1st canvas thread behind the other for the top edge. With double strands of black knitting worsted, work the edging stitch along this edge, being careful to use the 2 canvas threads as one. Fold the canvas at the next 2 free canvas threads for the bottom edge and complete as for top edge. Sew side seams with black knitting worsted.

**Center**

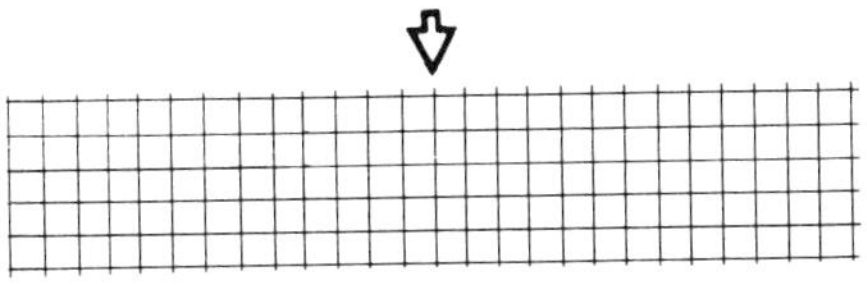

**Center monogram panel**

**COLOR KEY**

⊠ BLACK  ⎫
☐ GOLD   ⎬ HALF CROSS STITCH
⊡ FLAME  ⎭

A ⇨

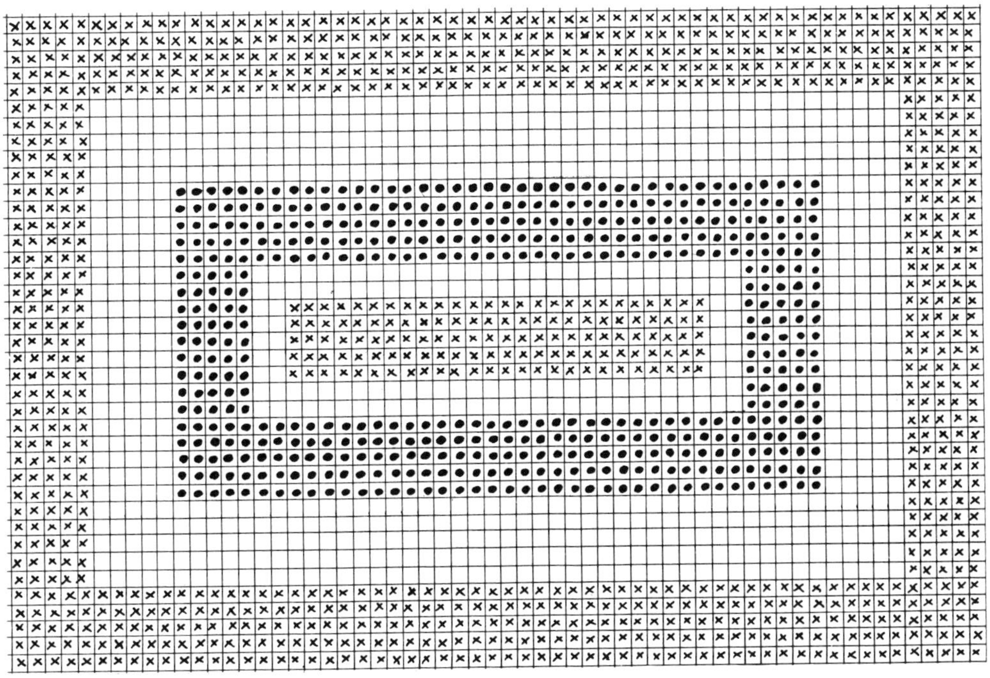

# Memo Pad

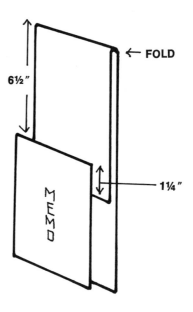

**← FOLD**

6½"

1¼"

## MATERIALS

6 yards of flame, 8 yards of black, and 9 yards of
    gold knitting worsted
1 6½ x 8½-inch piece of canvas
No. 18 tapestry needle
1 4½ x 20¾-inch piece of red felt
4 x 6-inch memo pad

For your working area, measure 1 inch down
from one short edge and 1 inch in from the adjacent long edge of canvas, and mark with a pin.
This is **A** on the Memo Pad Chart. "Memo" is
worked in cross stitch, and the remainder of the
design is worked in half cross stitch and each
stitch is worked over 1 thread of the canvas.
Work each row from left to right and turn the
canvas upside down at the end of each row.

Follow Color Key for colors and stitches and
starting at pin on canvas, follow chart to completion for design.

**Finishing:** Trim your canvas, leaving 5 canvas
threads free on each of the 4 sides. Place masking
tape on wrong side of each corner. Leaving 1
canvas thread free for the edge around the 4
sides of the embroidered piece, fold the raw
edges of the work to the wrong side, mitering the
corners. Pin in place. With double strands of
black yarn, work the edging stitch around the
outer edge, starting with Figs. 1, 2, and 3, then
repeating Figs. 2 and 3 alternately. Place narrow
edge of red felt 1¼ inch in from the top edge
to the wrong side of the embroidery, leaving the
remainder of the felt to extend beyond the top
edge. Sew the felt edge to the back of the canvas.
Fold the felt 6½ inches from the top of the embroidery to form the back, then bring the remainder of the felt over the back (for pocket) and
over the wrong side of the entire embroidered
piece. Pin in place. Whip-stitch edges of pocket
together. Sew lining in place on embroidered
piece. Make a 3⅞-inch slit 5⅞ inches up from
the bottom edge. Work a buttonhole stitch around
the slit. Insert pad.

A ⇨

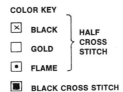

**COLOR KEY**

| | | |
|---|---|---|
| ⊠ | BLACK | ⎫ |
| ☐ | GOLD | ⎬ HALF CROSS STITCH |
| · | FLAME | ⎭ |

▣ BLACK CROSS STITCH

# Slip-Seat Chair Cover

*This piece measures approximately 18 inches square and is designed for a 14 inch-square chair seat, allowing 2 inches to tuck under each of the 4 sides. This is an average size. For a smaller seat, eliminate stitches and rows; for a larger seat, add stitches and rows.*

## MATERIALS

100 yards of orange, and 95 yards
    of coral heavy acrylic rug yarn
1 20-inch square of canvas
No. 18 tapestry needle
1 package double-fold bias tape

Run a basting thread through center of canvas, once from side to side and once from top to bottom, and around the outer edge of the desired size of your embroidered piece. The Slip-Seat Chair Cover Chart shows a center diamond, plus 1 diamond repeat to each side. The piece is worked in gobelin stitch and each stitch is worked over 8 threads of the canvas.

Following the Color Key and chart for Slip-Seat Chair Cover, start at center of piece where the basting stitches cross and work all blocks (4 stitches = 1 block) for the center diamond.

After completion of the center diamond, work the diagonal line pattern as shown on the graph, carrying each line to the basting thread around the 4 outer edges of the piece. Fill in the centers of each diamond motif in same manner indicated for the center diamond.

Sew bias tape over the edge of the piece, then mount the piece on the seat for which it was planned.

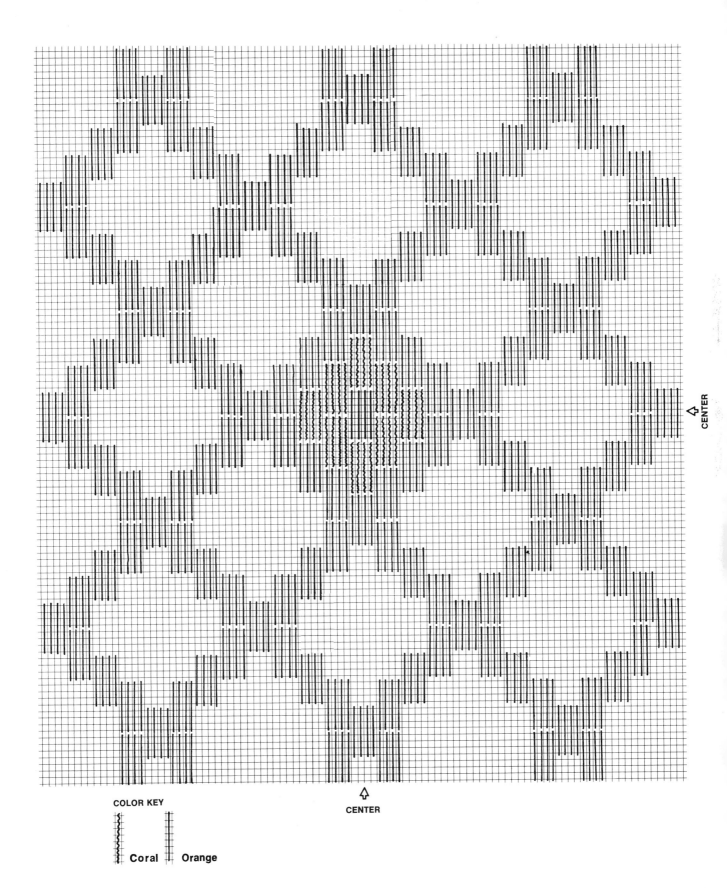

CENTER

CENTER

COLOR KEY

Coral    Orange

# Sampler

## MATERIALS

50 yards of gold, 35 yards of red, 25 yards of orange, and 10 yards of black knitting worsted or Persian wool

1 13 x 18-inch piece of canvas

No. 18 tapestry needle

Run a basting thread across the center of the canvas, once from top to bottom and once from side to side (point at which threads cross is marked on the chart by a diamond). Follow the Color Key and the chart for the Sampler. The letters, numbers, and dots are worked in cross stitch, the outlines and backgrounds of the center panel and the signature panels in half cross stitch, the border in gobelin stitch, and the edging in long-legged cross stitch.

Embroider the outline of the center panel (80 stitches across and 27 stitches high). Work the motto, then fill in the background with gold worsted or wool, working each row from left to right, and turning the work upside down at the end of each row. Work the alphabet, the numbers, and the dots. Outline this rectangle, then fill in the background with orange worsted or wool. Work the border background.

Following the Needlepoint Chart for the diamond, work the diamonds in alternating orange and red yarn, starting at top left with orange and working each of the two small orange diamonds along the short sides with 7 vertical gobelin stitches.

When diamonds have been completed, embroider 4 long self-color stitches over each diamond, each one from the center of the diamond to the middle of each of the 4 sides. Work a red French knot in the center of each orange diamond and an orange French knot in the center of each red diamond.

Outline each monogram and date panel. Fill in desired initials in top left and right panels and date in lower left and right panels, working the initials and dates in red, filling in the background in gold.

Work the edging in red long-legged cross stitch, using as the top row of the edges the same row of holes on the canvas as was used by the last row of the border. Work as shown in the stitch illustrations, repeating from 5 to 10 across the row. To end the row evenly, do not repeat 9 and 10, but work from **A** to **B**.

Block the finished piece and mount or frame as desired.

**COLOR KEY**

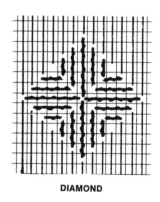

- RED HALF CROSS STITCH
- RED CROSS STITCH
- BLACK CROSS STITCH
- GOLD GOBELIN STITCH
- ORANGE GOBELIN STITCH

**DIAMOND**

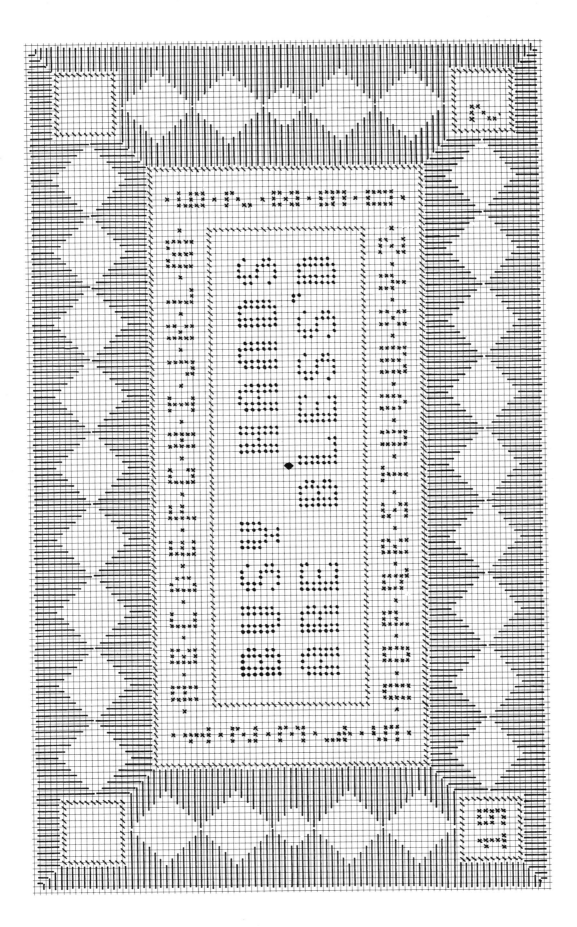

# 8

# Patchwork

The origin of patchwork is quite different from that of some of the more "frivolous" handcrafts, such as crewel embroidery and needlepoint which started and are still being worked purely as decorative art forms. By contrast, the thought of putting all kinds of little pieces together to form one large whole first came to the minds of those who were in need of very functional things such as covers to keep themselves warm with in bed and other large pieces that could be hung over windows and doors to keep out cold winter drafts.

Early American settlers had few opportunities for buying things, and it was they who thought of using still good bits and pieces from wornout clothing and other woven materials to make large crazy quilts, which was the name given to the first pieces of patchwork. As time went on, they became increasingly aware of how interesting this

type of work could be, and began making some very exciting designs with their little patches. Besides having the comfort of being able to fulfill their basic needs, they were now concerned with the esthetics of their skill and traded and shared their scraps with neighbors to get colors they didn't have, in order to enhance their patterns. All country fairs had displays and open competition for the most original and beautiful patchwork designs.

Interestingly, this simple handcraft has developed from a very humble and functional beginning to its great popularity as a recreational hobby today, when we can buy all the ready-made quilts and curtains we want, or certainly as many yards of material as we need to make our own, if we prefer to do so. There is fun and a real challenge, however, in one's reaching into

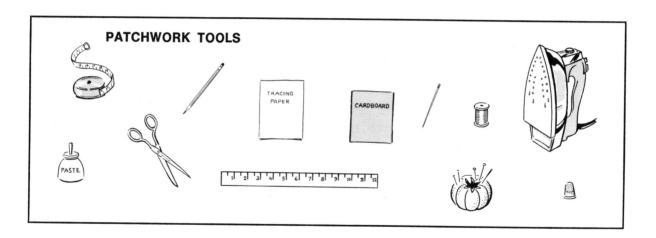

## PATCHWORK TOOLS

a scrap bag for different little pieces of material that will work together to form some interesting new creation. Patchwork designs are so in style today that there are many who, for the lack of a scrap bag, will buy small lengths of assorted materials to be able to create a patchwork effect on a bright high-fashion skirt or vest, or perhaps on a coverlet, tablecloth, or some other furnishing for their home.

Patchwork is easy to do, and the equipment needed is very simple and basic. You may make as few or as many patches as you wish at any one time, and you may work with them anywhere at all, for each patch is a small piece and easy to carry. We hope you will try some of the special things we've designed for you as a beginner, and that you will be happy in making them, either with your own leftover materials or with new ones that you've chosen to buy. If you enjoy sewing at all, you will probably find your greatest pleasure in this kind of work.

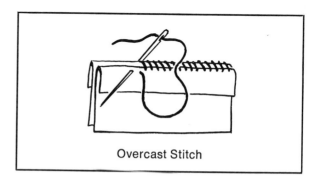

Overcast Stitch

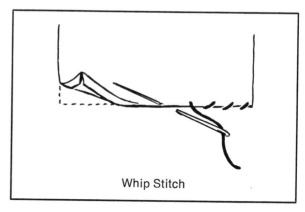

Whip Stitch

## PATCHWORK STITCHES

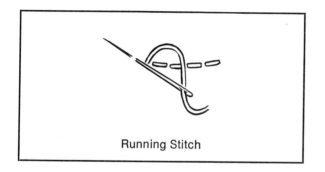

Running Stitch

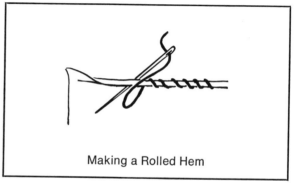

Making a Rolled Hem

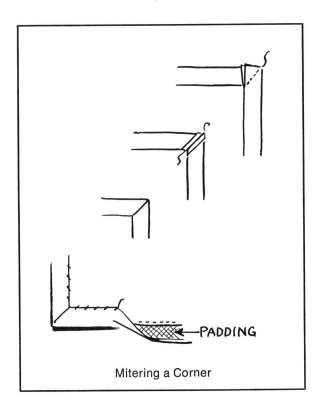

Mitering a Corner

## GENERAL INSTRUCTIONS

Assemble all your working materials before you start. Since many small pieces are involved in patchwork, it is advisable to keep them assorted in some way in a fairly large box, easy to keep organized, and easy to take out and put away at will.

Your scissors should be sharp. There is much cutting to be done, and sharp scissors will help you get a clean smooth edge on your pieces, rather than a ragged one or one that will easily ravel.

To make your pattern pieces, first trace off the unit you will be using along the solid line in the illustrations. Paste the cutout onto thin cardboard, and then cut the cardboard to use as the pattern when cutting your fabric. Make another pattern in the same manner for seam guidelines, this time tracing and cutting along the dotted lines. When fabric pieces are cut, center the 2nd pattern piece onto the wrong side of the fabric and trace around the entire outside edge. This guideline makes it easier to stitch one piece to another and gives a smooth finish to your work.

Cut all your pieces before starting a project. Your work flows more smoothly if you can keep on sewing once you've started, rather than having to stop to measure and cut more pieces.

Patch pieces may be machine-stitched or hand-stitched together, depending on the particular design being made. When stitching by hand, use a running stitch small enough so that your material does not pucker along the seams.

Press all your patchwork seams in one direction before adding your finishing touches.

# Apron

## MATERIALS

½ yard of white material (Color A), ¾ yard of red dotted print (Color B), and ½ yard of lining material in desired color; all 36 inches wide

Thread to match

Prepare the pattern pieces. Using the large piece, cut 16 pieces each of A and B, then reverse the pattern piece and cut another 16 pieces of each color. Mark your seam guidelines on the wrong side of each piece. Following the chart, stitch your pieces, right sides together, along the seam lines. Press all seams to one side.

Cut the lining material, using the apron as your pattern. Place the apron and the lining right sides together and stitch side and bottom edges, making a ¼-inch seam. Leave top edges free. Turn right side out. Gather the top of the piece together to measure 18 inches, sewing the apron and the lining together with a running stitch.

**Finishing: Top Band:** Cut a strip of B 18½ inches long by 4½ inches wide. Turn in each end ¼ inch to the wrong side and baste. Baste the band to the underside of the apron, having right sides together with gathers evenly spaced. Stitch in place with a ¼-inch seam, then pull out the basting thread. Turn in the ¼-inch seam allowance on the free edge, fold the band to the front of the apron and baste in place along the top, ¼ inch down from the edge. Stitch in place and remove basting thread. **Ties:** Cut 2 strips of B, each 24 inches long by 4½ inches wide. Roll a hem on the 1 short and 2 long edges of each tie by turning in ¼ inch to the wrong side, then ¼ inch again. Gather the unhemmed short edges to fit inside the open ends of the apron band, insert and stitch them in place ⅛ inch from band edge. Press the finished piece.

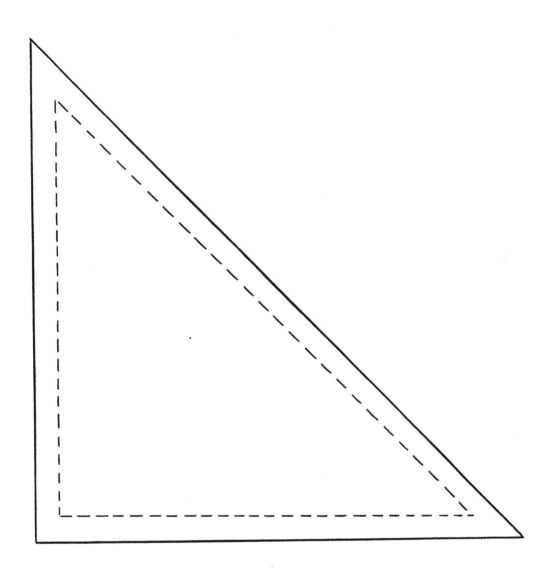

# Doggie Toy

## MATERIALS

¼ yard each of red dotted print (Color B), blue flowered print (Color C), and royal blue (Color D) 36-inch-wide material

Thread to match

Polyester fiberfill, foam rubber, or other stuffing material

¼ yard each of 1-inch- and 2-inch-wide white fringe

1 small red button

¾ yard of red grosgrain ribbon

Prepare the pattern pieces. Using the large piece, cut 18 pieces of B, 16 of C and 20 of D. Mark your seam guidelines on the wrong side of each piece. Following the chart, stitch 22 pieces, right sides together, along the seam lines for one side of the toy and make another piece in the same manner for the other side.

Cut 2 strips of D, each to measure 2½ inches wide and 26½ inches long and stitch together to form a strip 53 inches long. Pin this piece in place, right sides together, around one section

of the toy, starting and ending at underleg at point **X** on the chart. Stitch in place, making a ¼-inch seam. (If you are stitching by machine, when you come to a corner, leave the needle in your fabric, lift sewing foot, turn the fabric in position, lower sewing foot and continue to stitch.) Repeat around the other section of the toy in the same manner, starting at point **X** on the chart and ending at **XX**, leaving an opening. Turn right side out and stuff to desired firmness. Turn in raw edge on opening and whip-stitch in place.

Sew 5 (2 C and 3 D) of the remaining pieces together for the ear and the other 5 for the tail. Stuff each of these to desired firmness and whip-stitch in place, turning in the ¼-inch seam allowance.

**Finishing:** Sew button in place for nose. Cut and sew the 1-inch fringe in place for eyelashes as shown and place 2-inch fringe around nose as shown for whiskers. Tie ribbon into a bow around the neck.

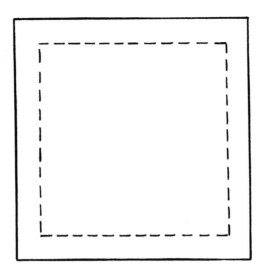

|   |   | C |   |   |   |
|---|---|---|---|---|---|
| B | D | B |   |   |   |
| C | B | D |   |   | C |
|   | D | B | D | B | C | B |
|   | C | D | B | C | D | C |
|   | B | C | xx |   | B | D |

# Pillow

## MATERIALS

⅓ yard each of red dotted print (Color B) and
　　royal blue (Color D) 36-inch-wide-material
Thread to match
15 small white tassels
Polyester fiberfill, foam rubber or other stuffing
　　material

Prepare the pattern pieces. Using the large pattern piece, cut 16 pieces each of B and D. Mark seam guidelines on wrong side of each piece.

**Triangle Puffs** (make 16): Stitch one B and one D piece together along the seam guidelines on the two long edges, right sides together. Turn the triangle right side out. Stuff to desired firmness. Turn in ¼-inch seam allowance and whip-stitch bottom edges together. Following the chart, stitch puffs together with an overcast stitch.

**Finishing:** Sew tassels onto the finished pillow as shown, one at top and one at each point of each B triangle.

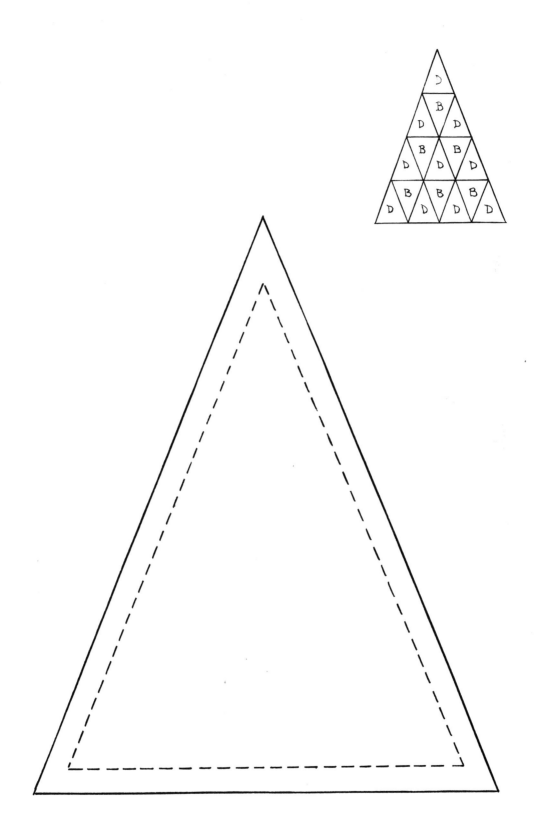

# Crib Coverlet

## MATERIALS

3 yards of white (Color A), ½ yard of 36-inch-wide red dotted print (Color B), ⅓ yard of blue flowered print (Color C), and 1½ yards of royal blue (Color D) 44-inch-wide material

Thread to match

Polyester fiberfill for stuffing

Prepare the pattern pieces. Using the large pattern piece, cut 291 pieces of A (96 for the coverlet top and 195 for lining), 39 of B, and 30 each of C and D. Mark seam guidelines on wrong side of each piece. **Square Puffs** (make 195): Using 1 each of the 195 A lining pieces and 1 each of the remaining 195 A, B, C, and D pieces, stitch them together along the seam guidelines on 3 sides, holding right sides together. Turn the squares right side out. Stuff to desired firmness. Turn in ¼-inch seam allowance and whip-stitch the 4th (remaining) edges together. Following the chart, whip-stitch the puffs together on the wrong side (lining side).

**Border:** From the remaining D material, cut 4 strips, each 49 inches long and 4½ inches wide, for the side borders, and 4 more strips, each 43 inches long and 4½ inches wide, for the top and bottom borders. Mark the center points of two side, top and bottom border strips, sides and top and bottom edges of the coverlet. Turning in ¼ inch on the border strips and matching center points, whip-stitch the borders in place to the top side edge of the coverlet. Miter the corners. Repeat with other border strips on the lining side of the coverlet. Cut strips of fiberfill to fit inside the border strips, and insert. Turn in ¼ inch along the open edges of the border and whip-stitch these edges together. Use a running stitch and matching thread to "quilt" around the border edge, ½ inch in from the edge.

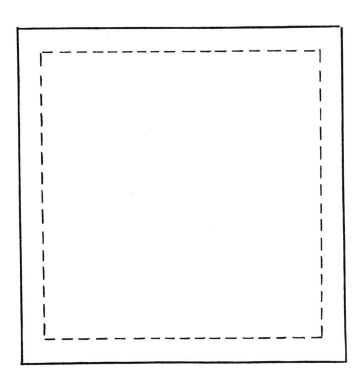

Repeat from 1 to 2

| 2 | | | | | 1 | | | | | | | | | |
|---|---|---|---|---|---|---|---|---|---|---|---|---|---|---|
| B | A | D | A | C | A | B | | | | | | | | |
| B | A | D | A | C | A | B | | | | | | | | |
| B | A | D | A | C | A | B | | | | | | | | |
| A | C | A | B | A | D | A | | | | | | | | |
| A | C | A | B | A | D | A | | | | | | | | |
| A | C | A | B | A | D | A | | | | | | | | |
| B | A | D | A | C | A | B | | | | | | | | |
| B | A | D | A | C | A | B | | | | | | | | |
| B | A | D | A | C | A | B | | | | | | | | |
| A | C | A | B | A | D | A | | | | | | | | |
| A | C | A | B | A | D | A | | | | | | | | |
| A | C | A | B | A | D | A | | | | | | | | |
| B | A | D | A | C | A | B | | | | | | | | |
| B | A | D | A | C | A | B | | | | | | | | |
| B | A | D | A | C | A | B | | | | | | | | |

# Index

**Notes**

# Notes

**Notes**

**Notes**

74 75 10 9 8 7 6 5 4 3 2 1